Displaced

The Journey Home

Tami Shaikh

ISBN-13: 9798409244163
ISBN-10: 1477123456

Cover design by: Art Painter
Library of Congress Control Number: 2018675309
Printed in the United States of America

This book is dedicated to the 100 million people worldwide who have been forcibly displaced from their homes.

And to those who dedicate their lives to helping others.

Contents

War

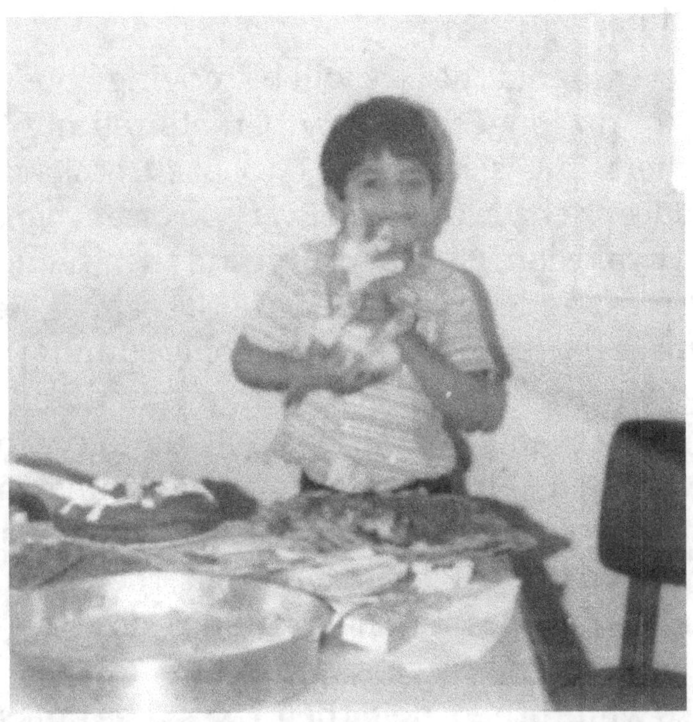

As the school bus drops me off after school, a man in a military uniform holding a gun, helps me cross the road. Once I reach the other side, I run toward my house where my mother is waiting for me. She looks worried and hugs me; it's as though she is relieved that I am home.

I ask my mother, "Who is that man?"

I really want to know because his uniform is

different from my father's. She looks scared and tells me he is an Israeli soldier and the southern part of my native country, Lebanon, has been occupied by the Israelis. I don't really understand what all that means, but I feel a sense of fear and uncertainty in the air.

And so, the journey for survival, of a four-year-old starts.

I am told that we will be moving houses because we are no longer safe. My parents tell my two older brothers, my sister, and I to pack basic necessities because we have to leave. Every so often, we hear a big loud explosion, people scream and then silence. We get in our car and are going toward the capital, Beirut. The scene still lives in my head—people running, militants everywhere, occasionally a large sound and then our car shakes, and my mother tells us to put our heads down. Even though the sun was shining in the sky, on the ground, it is like hell everywhere else. Where there used to be high rise buildings, there is only rubble that sits in piles on the ground. I also see Lebanese soldiers on the streets; some are standing on their tanks while others hold their rifles. The tanks look like big monsters, but little do I know that the men that cause the war are bigger monsters. We drive for a long time and see a house that looks deserted, and we run inside. There are already some squatters inside—a total of eleven people in a two-bedroom apartment. My bed is my mother's lap as we lie down on the floor; everyone sleeps wherever they find space. I can't sleep; even though I am only four, my brain knows something is truly wrong. I sense the extinction of the comfort and life I once knew; I smell horror and destruction. I know this is war. I watch my parents discuss our options—do we run, stay, or hide?

Today, thirty-six years later I finally feel settled. This country that has adopted me has given me protection, safety, and values me as a human being. I am currently a college professor, with endless possibilities ahead of me.

Thank you, Canada.

I am home.

--Giscard El Khoury

Prologue

I was sitting in my office finishing paperwork when the receptionist knocked on my door. I had explicitly asked her not to disturb me so I could finish my reports, but she had clearly disregarded my request.

"Yes?" I answered in an irritated tone I didn't use often.

"A family is here to see you."

"But I told everyone in the office I'm not seeing clients. I have to finish the reports."

"I'm sorry to disturb you, but they got agitated when I told them you weren't available. Would you please talk to them?"

I nodded, sighed, and turned the other way to roll my eyes. They were a young couple with three young children, maybe in their early thirties. The wife was wearing a traditional black *abaya*. The oldest daughter, who looked like she was around nine years old, wore a headscarf and big, round eyeglasses. She came in and stood quietly in the corner. The second was about five and had a sweet smile with long, thick eyelashes; she held onto a doll, not much bigger than a Barbie. The doll's face and clothes were dirty. The third was a baby who the mother was trying to breastfeed under her *abaya*. The father walked in with a bit of a limp; he held his wife's purse and another plastic bag filled with papers.

I motioned them to sit down. Then, once everyone was settled, I asked the first question I always asked, "How can I help you?"

In broken English, the husband started explaining how they

had left Syria and arrived in America on asylum but faced issues with their paperwork. I immediately knew I couldn't help and would have to refer them to someone else.

So, I smiled and, as usual, took out my referral list of places where they could go for assistance. I handed him the paper and said, "I'm so sorry; we can't help you here, but—"

"Please don't give us another list of addresses where we should go," cried the young mother. "Can't you just help?"

I felt as though someone had just slapped me across the face as my heart sunk from my chest into my stomach. I had no legal authority to help them, but in truth, my heart had grown numb after working with people who had paperwork issues for years. Their helplessness didn't seem to matter to me the way it used to. But in that moment, I felt ashamed. "I wish I could, but I don't have the expertise," I defended.

The mother continued to cry as the father said, "Everywhere we go, no one wants to help us. We don't know what to do anymore."

I felt sick to my stomach and turned around to call one of my attorney friends in hopes that they would talk to them. But, unfortunately somehow, I had become complacent and insensitive.

I worked as a citizenship coordinator for a non-profit organization in Orange County, California, which basically meant I helped people on their path to becoming US citizens. I mainly worked with LPRs (Green Card holders), but I also worked with attorneys to help refugees, asylees, and undocumented folks. Working with refugees and watching the horrific situation unfolded in the media was difficult for me. Most people only saw refugees as a faraway thing; however, in my line of work, I met them and heard their far too similar yet uniquely distinct stories every day.

Their stories often made me think of my father, who came to the US in the 1960s. Even though he wasn't a refugee, he left his country searching for a better life for himself. He understood the opportunities this would open for his children and for generations to come. On the other hand, my mother always wanted to move back to Pakistan because she didn't necessarily have to leave her country of birth. She was an immigrant, not a refugee; my mother had choices—she had a country to go back to. Pakistan was her love and home, and despite it being ravaged by religious fanatics, political mishaps, and a broken economic system, it was where her heart was. For her, she could never settle down in the US because it wasn't home, no matter how hard she tried to make it feel like it was.

The concept of having a home country never dawned on me. To me, home was wherever I felt happy and at ease. So, the country I was in never quite mattered. But I know I am privileged in where I stand, as my friends from Iraq, Afghanistan, and even Syria often call me lucky because I have a country to call home. For some of them, the country's political situation in which they live, has left them without passports.

Since I work in the nonprofit sector and have built relationships with organizations that work closely with refugees, I often receive messages requesting people to become foster parents to refugee kids who have lost their families to war. It was a horrible thought that some parents would send their children across the world just for a better life. Some parents set out to a better country that promised a better future for their children but never made it there alive. And so, the children in these circumstances often ended up alone, either in detention camps or foster homes. Many couldn't speak English and belonged to conservative religious backgrounds.

I met mothers who hadn't seen their parents, children, or siblings in years, and I have talked to refugee families who disclosed that they were living with ten to twelve other people in a one-bedroom apartment. Upon hearing such heartbreaking stories of desperate lives and desperate people searching for some sort of protection, I often wondered about those who weren't given asylum in other countries. My brain went on a downward spiral thinking about people who left their countries without knowing where they would end up. How do they knowingly leave everything behind and take their family into something that might cost them their lives? How does a parent put their child in so much danger? Then, an important question popped into my mind: Does a refugee ever feel like their new home is home? Unlike immigrants who *choose* not to return to their home countries, do refugees ever really accept their new country as home? I wanted to talk to refugees from around the world and find answers to my questions. Therefore, I decided to look for an organization with a rescue and response team that I could work with, so I could be in direct contact with refugees in hopes that they could help answer the endless stream of questions that I had.

When I decided to work on this project, it was supposed to be about the statistical and analytical aspects of the refugee crisis. I wanted to know why people leave their country, how they decide to just get up and go, where they get the money from, the economics behind starting a new life in a new country, and how the resettlement process happens. Yes, I wanted to know about the physical strain it takes, but I also wanted to inquire about the emotional and mental strain that this migration would take. My brain told me that it must be a horrible experience, but my heart believed that there had to be so little hope in these people's lives for them to risk everything in search of refuge in a new country. It was something I wanted to see for myself. I believed I had a heightened sense toward these people and could understand and write about their pain. I wasn't quite like them. I had never really witnessed war, nor did I have to leave everything behind and beg another country to take me in.

I spoke to many people as I marched forward with this project. Some wanted me to share their stories, while others didn't. Together, we walked through the trauma, laughed until our bellies hurt, and wiped each other's tears. Some grew annoyed by my constant questioning, while others were eager to build a life-long bond with me.

When I went to Greece, I believed that I would come back knowing more about the situation in Syria. I learned more about how many refugees are refugees and how the rescue teams help them. When I went to Nepal and met refugees from different countries, I learned why the Bhutanese left their country in the early 1990s. And my trip to the Pakistan-Afghanistan border taught me about the Soviet war and how many Afghans are undocumented in Pakistan.

However, where I initially expected to find answers, I only found more questions-questions about other people's inner anguish, human dynamics, the pain of displacement, sense of abandonment, the fear of death, political interests, and heavenly resilience.

War is something I have thought about extensively. My mother often told me about the Bangladesh Liberation war in 1971. I was six-months-old, and she was visiting Bahawalpur, Pakistan. At the time, we were living in Orange County, California. When they heard the sirens, she said they had to turn off all the lights and wait until the deafening sounds of the fighter jets above stopped. It's been almost fifty years since, and she still talks about it like it was yesterday. She returned to her comfortable home in Orange County right when the war ended. According to the UN, as many as three million people were killed during this war. My mother was one of the lucky ones.

War is haunting for those who have witnessed it. For others, the images and experiences of war have been so deeply embedded in their minds that it has become a familiar aspect of life. As a result, these people have stopped caring.

According to the *Human Security Report* by the United

Nations, war is defined as follows:

- A conflict is coded as a war when the battle-death toll reaches 1,000 or more in a given calendar year.
- An extrastate armed conflict is between a state and an armed group outside the state's own territory. These are primarily colonial conflicts.
- An interstate armed conflict is a conflict fought between two or more states. An intrastate armed conflict (also known as a civil conflict) is a conflict between a government and a non-state group that takes place largely within the territory of the state in question.
- An intrastate armed conflict becomes an internationalized intrastate armed conflict when the government, or an armed group opposing it, receives support in the form of troops from one or more foreign state(s).

War causes the displacement and migration of millions. According to the UNHCR, 68.5 million people are currently displaced worldwide. About twenty-five million are refugees, in which more than 50% are under the age of eighteen. In addition, there are also about ten million stateless people who have been denied nationality and do not have access to fundamental human rights like education, healthcare, and employment.

According to the UNHCR, the major source countries for refugees are:

Syrian 6.8 million

Venezuela 4.6 million

Afghanistan 2.7 million

South Sudan 2.4 million

Myanmar 1.2 million

Part One

Pak/Afghan Border

Aziz always wanted to be a poet, so I asked him to write something for me.

"But my English isn't good."

"Don't worry about it; just write from your heart," I replied.

"You know *dokhtar* (daughter), I always wanted to be a famous poet like Khushaal Khatak, but life has been so difficult."

"Did you write when you were young?"

Aziz paused for a moment, wiped his eyes, and answered, "I was never really able to tell anyone in my family about it; I always had to be a man. I would make up love poems for my wife, but she was not educated, so she didn't understand their depth. She did not appreciate my intricate use of language and the way I wove words together so beautifully."

"Did you save the poems?" I felt stupid as soon as I asked the question. He had fled Afghanistan during the war; obviously, he did not have them. "I'm sorry."

"Can you help me write the poem for your book?" he asked excitedly.

Anyone who knows me or has ever read my work knows that poetry most definitely isn't my strong suit; I can't write it or understand it; in fact, I don't even like it. Still, I nodded my head and wondered what the hell I was going to do.

Aziz came up with the poem himself and first wrote it in

Dari. He then wrote it in paragraph form in English, periodically looking up from his paper to ask me how to say certain words.

Once he was done, he inquired about its structure. I told him to structure it in any way that worked for him. And so, his final product was as follows:

Burning Land

journeying towards

the waters of inferno

Burn, burn, burn

the vultures will watch me

he is shocked at the

lies that these men will tell

I look at the horizon but

there are only clouds

Far, far, far

clouds have appeared by

fires made by minds

domicile to me is long gone

in a treasure box of memory

It doesn't stand like the vultures

Fly, fly, fly

but falls to pieces like me

my wife wails, and I am brave to

keep the virtue of my manhood

alive my boy and girl run wildly

in a circle like bats, they bump into

the walls not knowing what they want

Run, run, run

but they follow me, and I

don't know what to do

the bombs, smoke, bullets, and dying

people

No one hears me in this land of war

Silence, silence, silence

I am nullity and naked

a creature that preys just like the bird.

Aziz passed away in 2019. He was 73 years old.

Pakistan is located in Southeast Asia and borders Afghanistan, Iran, India, and China. My connection to this beautiful country is deeper as my ancestors are from Pakistan. In 1965, my parents moved to the US, where my father attended UCLA. He experienced a culture shock as he tried to adapt to life in Los Angeles.

I was born in Santa Monica, but my parents decided to move back to Pakistan when I was seven years old. So, when I was nineteen, I moved back to Southern California. Growing up in Pakistan during the '80s was an interesting era in itself. I was already an *angrez*—according to all the school bullies—which translates to a western foreigner. To me, and I'm sure to all those who referred to me by this name, it was an insult.

I distinctly remember watching the country change during my time there—something that my young mind felt and internalized but did not verbalize until many years later. The media became stricter about requiring newscasters to cover their heads, and the rise of Islamism was evident. Suddenly, numerous men were walking around with bright green turbans—the sign of a *jihadi* or member of the Taliban. Zia-ul-Haq was the president of Pakistan at the time and he had overthrown Zulfiqar Ali Bhutto in martial law and became the head of the army and the country. He brought in Islamic laws, rooted the educational curriculum in Islamic teachings, and funded thousands of *madrassas* (fanatic religious schools) all over the country. He also appointed Islamists into the judiciary, military, and heads of many government-run organizations.

Backed by the US and Saudi Arabia, Zia-ul-Haq assisted and trained the Afghan *mujahidin* against the Soviet Union's occupation and eventually their withdrawal. The Soviet-Afghan war that went on from 1979 to 1989 left many civilians fleeing Afghanistan. During that time, hundreds of thousands of Afghans moved through the open borders and still live as refugees in Pakistan today.

Now, Afghanistan is a country that is ravaged by war and terrorism, but it has a rich historical background. It's a landlocked country that sits at the entrance to Southeast Asia and was an important trade route for merchants coming from Europe. Many rulers and conquerors tried and succeeded in ruling this precious piece of land that is almost the size of Texas. Alexander the Great conquered it in 329 BC, and Mahmud of Ghazni was the first independent ruler to the land that would later be called Afghanistan. Genghis Khan also conquered the land during the thirteenth century.

By 1870, Afghanistan had been governed by many Arab rulers who brought Islam to the region. The British fought three wars with the Afghans during the nineteenth century and didn't win any. Finally, in 1933, Afghanistan had a new king, Zahir Shah, who brought stability and prosperity to the region for forty years.

In 1978, the conservative, extremist Muslims began a guerrilla movement and called themselves the Mujahadeen. Then, in 1979, the USSR invaded Afghanistan. The Afghan civilians struggled with attacks from the Soviets and the Mujahadeen, who later morphed into al-Qaida, which means "the leaders." Osama bin Laden led the Taliban, backed by the US, Britain, and China, who sent ammunition to them through Pakistan.

In 1982, over four million Afghans fled to neighboring countries. About 2.8 million went to Pakistan through the open borders, and another 1.5 million migrated to Iran. Currently, there are about 1.3 million registered refugees in Pakistan, and about one million are thought to be undocumented, according to UNHCR. Pakistan, a new country that gained its independence from the British rule and separated from India in 1947, was then overpowered by the entry of millions of Afghan refugees after the Soviet war.

***

My father loved to travel.

Growing up, he always took us on vacations. My parents would put us in the car that was packed with snacks and sandwiches and drive to closer destinations, or we would have our yearly international vacation that was even farther and far more exciting.

Sometimes, we visited a city called Peshawar, which lies on the Pakistan-Afghanistan border. This ancient city has a history that ranges back to 500 BC. It is simultaneously historical, beautiful, and frightening. The mountain ranges surrounding it were beautiful, and funny enough, some were lush green while others were sandy and dirty. The shade of green that enveloped the mountains was different from where I lived, and I wondered how so many kinds and colors of grass could even exist. The sky was always clear, and there was no pollution in the air. The ponds were a turquoise blue, and the water was freezing all year round. Random breathtaking waterfalls showed up every few miles. Goats and cows grazed on the edge of the mountain showing their familiarity with the terrain and causing extreme excitement in our young brains. We talked about racing a four-legged creature up the hill, knowing all too well that we would not stand a chance. We stayed in a rest house, which was essentially the same as staying in an Airbnb. At the time, there were not any big hotel chains or resorts. These rest houses had cooks and cleaners, and so, we would let them know what we wanted to eat, and they would prepare it for us. The food was fantastic, and I often munched on the famous chapli kababs and Afghani rice, which were always our family favorites.

My mother loved shopping whenever we visited this city because the *Pathans* (locals) brought silks from China to sell for great prices. She often purchased pure silk that felt like the softest fabric I had ever touched. She haggled with the storekeepers, accusing them of not giving her the best silk. When they would swear on their life that it was, she would ask them to burn a corner of the fabric to make sure it was pure. Although I am not entirely confident this is true—pure silk doesn't immediately catch fire. Instead, it turns black and twists at the corners. And so, after confirming the authenticity of her purchase, she would go forth to purchase dozens of different colors and materials and fabric to gift my extended family upon return.

The women of Peshawar were beautiful; they did not look like other Pakistani women. Most had very light skin, blue or green eyes, and appeared more European than South Asian. It was a different world that contradicted itself in many ways. The men were primarily handsome, but they carried rifles and had long unruly beards. It was an area of visible exquisiteness, but the tribal rigidness and religious fanaticism were obvious. The prevalent language of that area was Pashto. They spoke Urdu, the national language of Pakistan, with a distinct accent.

My fascination with this place began when I was young. Peshawar was the door from where millions of refugees entered Pakistan. It was where UNHCR started the first refugee camps in the early 1980s. Returning after so many years was bittersweet. But this time, I did not go to the border; I went to the camps where people had been living since the early 1980s. From Peshawar, many of them were brought to Rawalpindi.

When I started to work on this project, I always wanted to interview the refugees in Pakistan. It was like I knew these people already, despite speaking a different language and being from a foreign country. Luckily, one of my cousins worked for UNHCR in Pakistan, and he connected me with the necessary people that could help me get involved in the work. I spoke with a gentleman named Qaisar Khan Afridi of UNHCR, who helped organize all the interviews. I dragged my mother along, as she has been my role model in her charity work. I figured if I got tongue-tied for some reason, she could take over the conversation.

We decided to head there early in the morning and return later that same day rather than spending the night. The driver picked us up at around 6:00 a.m. Driving through the highways in Pakistan brought back so many memories for me: the nearly paved roads, the plains of the Punjab, mustard fields, and the mud houses along the route. Cows walked around aimlessly on green fields, eating away at the shrubs.

The camp was located outside a city called Rawalpindi, about 350 km from Lahore, where my parents live. We drove for about four hours and finally reached our meeting place with the representatives from the UNHCR. They told us to stop in front of a university to lead us to a tiny road to the camps.

Once we pulled in, we waited for the jeep that would take us to the camps; my anxiety returned. Once again, a million questions popped into my head. I hoped I would be able to do their stories justice.

Even though I had traveled to many other countries and talked to many refugees, I felt a special kinship with these people. The Pashtuns are known to be extremely warm and hospitable; they would give their lives for friends. But then, they were also known to be passionate in their love and hate toward others. I was not sure if I would understand the language, but one thing I knew for sure was that culturally, they would be a lot more like the kind of people I had grown up around.

I brought my attention back to my surroundings in hopes of silencing my screaming thoughts for just a short while. The road had started out as a two-way street and slowly turned into a narrow, muddy, and broken one. There was only enough room for one car to pass at a time, as each driver avoided big rocks and potholes ahead. It had rained a few days before, so there were puddles littered everywhere. Our car jumped around as the driver tried to swerve between the hazards. We only saw dark clouds, barren land, and electric poles for a while. The wires were hanging over the muddy slough. Then, suddenly, I started to see signs of life; little kids played tag, jumped in puddles, and a few older ones sat on the ground chatting away. They were all boys.

Then, the tiny mud houses started to appear. They were lined up perfectly, yet the way the houses were made was chaotic. They were constructed from mud with pieces of cloth hanging in the place of doors; some huts had hay on the roof while fragments of pipes stuck out on others. There were animals, chickens, and cows running around or chewing away lazily.

The Jeep in front of us stopped, and so, we stopped, too. We hopped out of the car and walked toward the team from UNHCR. There were two men and two women; one of them was my contact with whom I had organized the trip. We greeted each other. The head of the group, Qaisar, told us that we would head off to one of the elder's house because all the women went there to chat. The two women from the UNHCR agreed to help with translation and would accompany us on our journey. Since the women of the camps uncovered their faces and heads, they would speak freely if it was all women.

The elder whose house we were going to talked to my chaperones before motioning us to follow him. There was no gate or entrance; we walked straight into a narrow path that was uneven and had puddles of water like the rest of the land. We finally arrived at the house where we would sit and chat. There were no doors, so the camp elder held up the torn, white fabric that hung in place of one, and our chaperones walked in as we followed closely behind.

It was a courtyard in the middle with rooms around it. On the left side, the land was raised, and there were two cows and five goats. Two of the goats were wearing children's jackets—they even had their limbs in the arms of the jacket.

About four to five women came out of the room and greeted us. They spoke all at once in loud voices and had the biggest smiles plastered on their faces. Each one hugged me and smiled. There were lots of children, primarily girls, running around, laughing, and playing. The house seemed to have a life of its own.

Our chaperones asked us to take off our shoes before entering the room. And so, I bent down to slip off my boots and nearly tripped when a young girl standing behind me put her hand on my back to keep me upright. We both looked at each other and smiled. At that moment, I felt like everything was going to be okay.

I entered slowly and took in my surroundings. The room was about 200 to 300 square feet. Big trunks were stacked on top of each nicely on one side of the room, with quilts and comforters neatly folded on top.

The rest of the room had no furniture; the floor was covered with a dark red carpet that had an interesting square design stitched into its fibers. Each square contained a yellow flower—like the mustard flowers we had seen on our drive there. Necklaces made of plastic garlands usually worn during weddings or when inviting someone as a chief guest were hung on the walls. We sat down on the cushions that lined three of the room's walls, and the room started to fill up with women and children of all ages.

The women wore their traditional Afghan outfits that consisted of a long, embroidered dress with beads called a *kameez,* and loose and baggy pants, called *shalwar.* On their heads, they wore scarves that hung loosely on both sides with their long hair pulled in the front. Some had braids. Most of the ladies wore long necklaces made from turquoise and red beads. They were beautiful women with coral-colored cheeks, bright eyes, and generous smiles.

As we began the interviews, I noticed one boy around fifteen years old sitting among the women. I was a bit surprised because usually, once boys are twelve years old, they are considered men and stay away from the women's quarters. However, the boy appeared as though he had a mental challenge, as the mother ensured he sat close to her and ran her fingers through his hair every time he got upset or fussy.

The moment we sat down, one of the ladies brought filled with cookies. Another brought tea in glass cups with pitcher's underneath. The tea was a different color from what we are used to having; it didn't look like black or green tea—it was something in the middle, but it tasted delicious and had lots of sugar in it.

Once we started to sip our hot tea, our chaperone spoke to the ladies in the language, asking if we could record the interview. All the ladies in attendance agreed, as long as no photos or videos of their faces were taken. When my interpreter posed one of the questions I had prepared for the interview, the women began speaking all at once, forcing the translator to interject and slow them down every now and then. She would stop after every answer and translate it for me to audio record and then ask them the next question. Most questions were answered by the wife of the elder whose house we were in.

Tell me about your journey coming to Pakistan.

We left Afghanistan about thirty-five years ago. My son was four-months-old, and now he is almost thirty-six. We came from a little village where we used to take care of our animals. We were farmers and lived peacefully. Then, suddenly, there were the Russians attacking us from the sky, and bombs fell from every direction. On the ground, the Taliban started attacking. We decided that we had to leave Afghanistan and head for Pakistan, so we collected our things and animals. I was very young and had a baby; I left with my husband and his family. We were a big group of people along with our animals. We walked to the border and then stayed in the camps until things got better in Afghanistan. We planned to come back home. We never thought that we would lose our land, which meant everything to us.

We traveled at night and hid during the day because the Soviet jets threw bombs on anyone they saw. We traveled with camels and donkeys and let the elderly and kids ride them while we younger folk walked. It took us around forty days to finally reach the border, and we entered the city of Peshawar in Pakistan. We stayed in the camps in Peshawar for about ten to fifteen years, and then came to Rawalpindi.

Would you go back to Afghanistan if you could?

Since I came here, I do not know anything about my family back home. I do not know if my parents or siblings or anyone for that matter is still alive; sometimes, I think maybe they are somewhere in Pakistan also. But I do not know. I came with my husband's family, so I left my whole family back in Afghanistan. I try not to overthink it too much, as this is our home now. Our children were born here and are now getting married. This is home for all of us. I know we will die here.

How do you earn a living?

Our men make money by buying fruits and vegetables from the farmers and selling them at the local markets or on the side of the road. We try to help by sewing and making jewelry. Sometimes people like you come around, and we can make some money to help. But our job is to take care of the children, our husbands, clean, and cook.

Do you miss Afghanistan?

Some days I do dream of when I was younger and living in the fields of Afghanistan, but what is the use now? I am old, and I am not going anywhere. Today, my son is thirty-four years old; he is a grown man with a family of his own.

We stopped for a bit. A young lady brought in a box and started to pull out cushion covers that she made and sold. They were brightly colored with even more brilliant embroidery and lots of gold tassels. She told us that it was traditional to give a bride these cushions for her wedding, so she made and sold them. Then, other women began bringing in necklaces for sale. Some were just like the ones they were wearing—the big turquoise and red beaded ones—while others brought necklaces made from tiny, colorful beads with lots of different patterns.

My mother and I bought about eight necklaces in total.

After we completed our purchases, another lady came forward and started to tell us her story. She was related to the lady we had previously spoken to, and she asked if she could tell her story too. I was thrilled.

How did you get here?

Our husbands were brothers, and we came together. We have traveled our journey together since we were young girls; why would we want things to change now? We arrived in six days and seven nights because we did not stop. Our family continued the journey during the day, despite the bombing and the Taliban fighters. But God protected us, and we reached our destination.

Do you like living here?

Pakistan has welcomed us, and this is our home. No matter what people say, we have found happiness in these camps. We live like a big family—sometimes we fight, and other times we are good to each other. The only issue here is our families are growing, and it is becoming more and more congested. Before, we had two or three people living in one house; now, we have twelve to fifteen. But it is just that our families are getting bigger, but the space for us in this world is still the same.

Do you think you would ever go back?

I do not think we could ever go back to Afghanistan. When my son shows me pictures and videos, we see destroyed buildings, and we do not recognize anyone. If we did go back, we would not even know who our friend is and who our enemy is. Are the Taliban helping us or destroying us? Does the government care about us or not? We would not know anything. Some days I have nightmares, and I remember the bombs falling and how scared we used to be.

When I asked one of the younger girls what she felt about living in the camps, she answered:

I was born in these camps, and to me, this is home. I do not feel like there's anything wrong with living here. I have never been to Afghanistan, and now when we see pictures, I cannot even imagine my life there. My mother sometimes tells me about how life used to be back in the Afghani village that we lived in. But I am glad that we came here because I have cousins and friends, and this is my life. I am going to get married next month, and I'm excited about my new life. And if I were given a chance to go back, I don't think I would. Why would I go back even to visit? I don't know anyone there. Pakistan is my home—now and always.

An older lady came forward who looked a little different from the others; she was darker and skinnier. Her silver hair shone from the rims of her scarf, indicating that she must have been around sixty. I found my eyes wandering in her direction a few times while the other ladies spoke.

And so, I turned to her and asked:

What do you wish for your future generations? Do you want them to go back or stay here?

My only wish for my children is that they get an education. Sadly, the camp only has one school that teaches kids in the primary section. The boys can go far away to study, but we don't send the girls far as they will get married anyway. I hope that if they can't get worldly education, they can get a religious education.

When I asked the ladies if they felt discriminated against by the locals, another told me:

We hardly go out and spend time with locals. There is a little supermarket on the campgrounds, so we buy whatever we need from there. If we need something else, our men usually bring it from outside of the camps. The only place where we meet and interact with locals is at the public hospitals as and when needed.

We are mistreated when we go there. The hospital officials push us, call us derogatory names, and treat us badly. They can tell by how we speak and dress—or maybe it's because we don't speak Urdu. They just don't like us. I learned a little bit of Urdu when my mother-in-law was in the hospital for many months. But when she passed away and I came back home, I forgot it because no one spoke Urdu around me. We are Pashtuns; our language is Pashto.

The interpreter relayed my request for a collective photo for my own personal keepsakes, and all the women agreed. They wrapped their scarves a little tighter and most covered their faces. Then, my mother and I got up and walked outside where children ran, played, cried, and laughed; one child was even pulling a goat's tail. As we stood outside the elder's house, one of the ladies kept telling us about her family. The stories were endless, and I was still trying to process it all. As we walked through the muddy pathway to our car, so many thoughts ran through my brain.

Once we finished talking with the refugees, I sat down with my chaperone/interpreter in hopes of getting to know her better. I was impressed with the way she interacted with the women. Mushayyadah was friendly and firm, and when they all started talking simultaneously, she knew exactly what to do to ensure we got the correct answers. I wanted to talk to this young lady about her work with UNHCR.

Tell me about yourself.

My name is Mushayyadah Gul; I joined UNHCR in 2010. I am from Peshawar. I have an MBA, a master's in political science, and LLB.

Why did you decide to do this work with UNHCR?

It was a dream to work with the United Nations but working with UNHCR is something different. It's a whole different kind of work. Getting to work with communities in need of help and those displaced for decades gives true satisfaction.

What is your fondest memory of working with refugees?

It's always lovely to see the happiness on people's faces when I can help them. One of my favorite moments was when a girl was returning to Afghanistan. She left her exit permit and was at the airport for her 2:00 a.m. flight. Suddenly, I got the call at around midnight. She was freaking out. I told her not to worry, ran to pick up the document, and headed over to the airport. When I handed it to her, she was so happy that she started crying with joy. Those are the moments that bring me so much happiness and make me believe that I am doing the right thing.

How do you plan to raise awareness in your community about the refugee crisis?

Raising awareness is something that needs to be done at a global level. To feel sensitivity toward refugees or other marginalized communities, we need to feel like them, be with them, listen to them, know their priorities, and think about what we can do to improve their lives. The world needs more empathy to understand and feel the pain of these people.

If there was one thing you could change about the world today, what would it be?

Percipience, because if you can empathize with others less fortunate than you, the world can be a peaceful place.

***

Part Two

Greece

"I miss home a lot. I did not really have any toys, but there was a mobile that my sisters and I had to share. So, I never really got to play on it, but here everyone has one. I really miss playing with my cousins; I even miss my aunt hitting me with a stick when we would be naughty. I definitely miss my grandmother's cooking. She died a few months before we left; I wish she were here, and then I would be thrilled.

"America is a friendly country, but I feel different than the other kids, and they look and treat me differently too. Everyone in my family looks sad. So, I just pray to Allah that we can all be happy and make this our home again."

~Abdirahim, ten-year-old Somali refugee living in Greece

When thinking of refugees, the country that came to my mind was Greece. I had witnessed the atrocities that were taking place on television numerous times, and often, Greece was focused on and discussed in extensive detail. I had many questions and knew the answers might not even be available to me. I tried to conduct online research on the topic, but I never stumbled on anything tangible or concrete. The only thing I learned was that the EU made a deal with the Greek government to keep all refugees in camps until they were given asylum in other countries.

And so, that was my next destination.

I decided to search for an organization with a rescue and response team with which I could work. Now that I had met people living in refugee camps for over forty years, I wanted to meet the ones coming off the boats—also known as the newly made refugees. After a bit of research, I came across an organization called Chios Eastern Shore Response Team that helps refugees as they arrive in Chios, Greece. The refugee camps

I first heard of them through a good friend of mine who had worked closely with the organization. It was the summer of 2017 and I had just started my MFA at Chapman University. I was searching for a topic for my dissertation that had to be approximately a hundred and fifty pages. My curiosity about refugees led me toward the idea of focusing on and funneling my knowledge and passion about refugees into a book for my dissertation. This book would have three purposes:

1) It would create awareness about the crisis

2) It would answer many of my own questions about home and what we as humans consider to be home

3) It would fulfill the needs and requirements of my MFA dissertation.

I was lucky to be surrounded by many supportive people and to have been given the funds by Chapman University to help with my travel goals.

I contacted them and finally saved enough money in the summer of 2017 to volunteer for three weeks. However, by the time I got all my paperwork together, the organization had enough volunteers and rejected my application. I sighed and believed that it simply just wasn't meant to be. I told myself I could use the money to go on vacation instead.

However, by September 2017, the organization contacted me in hopes that I could volunteer with them in winter of 2018, and so, my journey toward the answers I was searching for had finally begun.

I left for Athens on January 1st, 2018. It was definitely an interesting way to start off the year. My friend, Ana, and I stayed in Athens for about a day when we arrived, then headed for Chios, where the second biggest refugee camp that had just shut down was located. We left for Chios on January 3rd, 2018. We could have taken an eight-hour ferry ride, but instead, we decided to fly. I felt like my head was going to explode from a mixture of fear, insecurity, and excitement. Somewhere in the swirl of emotions, I also felt like a hero.

The flight was only around forty-five minutes, and when we landed, it was pouring rain out and the wind was strong enough to knock us off our feet. It was the tiniest airport I had ever seen —and I had seen some very small ones in Pakistan. Most of the passengers tried to enter the airport through one door; the rest of us were drenched—the rain hitting us in the face—while waiting for our turn.

Finally, Ana and I entered the airport and sighed in unison. We were soaking wet, so we took a moment to wipe our faces with the wet sleeves of our coats. I looked around the airport which consisted of two rooms—one for arrivals and the other for departures. The room for arrivals was small with a luggage belt running through the middle of it. About thirty of us huddled around it, making the tiny room feel even smaller.

While patiently waiting for our suitcases to tumble down the conveyor belt, I observed the other passengers, most of whom appeared like locals and were busy chatting away or lost on their phones. From where I stood, I could see the departure area on the other side of a wall with a huge opening between the two areas. I noticed two or three check-in counters and an additional waiting area. I finally saw my suitcase and grabbed it, soaking wet, as I pulled it off the belt and dragged it to the corner of the room. I wiped my wet hands on my jacket and called the lady who runs the organization to ask if she had sent someone to pick Ana and me up.

Toula immediately dialed a number into the phone and handed it to me. "Hello, Tami," she said.

"Hi, Toula," I heard on the other end of the incredibly loud phone. "We have arrived at the airport. Is someone here to pick me up?" I was growing impatient and irritated.

"I am sorry. We won't be able to come; a boat arrived this morning at 6:00 a.m. carrying forty refugees, and all the volunteers are there helping."

"Oh!"

"You can easily get a taxi from the airport."

"So, where should I tell the taxi to go?" I was nervous.

"Once you are in the taxi, call me, and I will tell the driver."

The other end fell silent. I don't know where my compassion had gone, but I was feeling more and more frustrated as I lugged my wet twenty-eight-inch suitcase in a crowded room where people looked at me, but no one offered to help. We finally got outside and stood under the little shade where rain wouldn't drench me, along with about ten other people. I saw a group of old cars parked on the far-right corner of the parking lot. It was pouring, and I wasn't sure if what I had spotted across the street was the taxi stand, so I went inside the airport again to ask the security guard. "Excuse me, where are the taxis?" I spoke.

A huge, friendly smile grew on his face. He was a tall man with a big, thick mustache and an even bigger protruding belly. "You need taxi? Let me call for you. Wait here; don't go outside."

I finally felt a little more relaxed. He spoke in Greek on his phone for a few minutes, then turned to me and said, "My friend Alessandro will take you. Let me help you with your suitcase."

He grabbed my suitcase, and we walked to a brown Nissan parked out front. The guard gestured for me to wait. Alessandro had an umbrella, and after putting my suitcase in the trunk, he handed it to me then ran back to the car. We slowly walked down the steps and sat in the backseat. Alessandro was a younger man with tiny eyes and a crooked nose.

"Where you go?" asked Alessandro. "I charge twenty euros anywhere on the island you go."

As though twenty euros was expensive, but we were exhausted at that point and simply nodded my head. "Let me call my friend; she will tell you," I replied.

I hurriedly dialed Toula's number and asked her to share the location I was meant to travel to with the drive. I handed the phone to him; he took it from me and spoke. Only a few moments after, he handed the phone back to me and looked at me oddly through his rearview mirror. We finally drove off, and I saw narrow streets, small colorful homes, and lots of stray cats and dogs. We drove right next to the beach, which was stunning. The water was turquoise, and the rain poured so beautifully into it. The clouds were dark, but the color of the water was unfazed by the darkness that covered it from above. When lightning struck, it reflected into the sea as if the surface had been replaced by a mirror. It was the most haunting yet stunning sight I had ever seen.

Alessandro stopped in front of a broken-down warehouse that was right next to the beach. The windows were cracked with graffiti all over them; the yellow paint was peeling off the building, and the wooden front door was closed. Two cars were parked in front.

As soon as we stopped, a beautiful lady opened the door and stepped out. She was my age and had brown hair piled above her head with a cigarette in one hand and an umbrella in the other.

She called out to me. "Tami, come in. Hurry before the rain comes inside."

I paid Alessandro, and he took my suitcase and ran toward the warehouse. We got out, I protected my laptop with a plastic bag and ran inside, too. As I brushed the rain off, Toula walked up and gave me a big hug.

"Thank you, honey, for coming. We are so happy to have you. Have a seat next to the heater. Everyone will be here soon."

After we ended our hug, I looked around. It was a large warehouse with boxes everywhere. In the middle was an area that was slightly raised, like a stage.

Around five or six long wooden benches were situated at each corner and in the middle was a table with oranges, chips, juice, water, and cigarettes. I left my suitcase in the corner and decided to explore. Toula stayed outside as more voiced echoed throughout the warehouse. I assumed others had arrived.

I walked to the far-right corner and discovered stairs going down to what looked like a bathroom. There was a line of huge, open crates that were separated and marked as *girls' jumpers 1-5 years*; *boys' t-shirts 1-5 years*; *men's hats and gloves*; *women's leggings*, and so on.

Four women and six men of all age groups and nationalities entered the warehouse. Everyone sat down, and I awkwardly walked toward the benches to join them. Toula sat in the front with three other people. She held a whiteboard that was divided into sections:

On-call one

On-call 2 + food

On-call 3 + tea

CH - Morning Afternoon

WH - Morning Afternoon

NPH - Morning Afternoon

Everyone smiled at me, and Toula introduced me as the new volunteer.

"Tami is a writer," she stated. "If you want to share your story with her, go ahead."

I smiled awkwardly and the meeting continued. They discussed the landing that had happened that morning and how the refugees waded through the Aegean Sea in the pouring rain because their smuggler dropped them off far away from the coast. There were twenty women, sixteen men, and four children—all from Syria. The volunteers touched on the fact that it was so difficult to see them walk through the cold sea while rain poured from above, but they couldn't go in the water and help them as the police wouldn't allow it. So, they watched helplessly as families tried to reach the shore. One volunteer began to cry as she talked about the little girl that was shivering even after they had given her warm clothes and food. At that moment, I felt so ashamed of myself for being upset that no one came to pick me up from the airport.

Then, they started asking for volunteers to fill the shifts that were printed on the board Toula was still holding up. One by one, they filled in their names. I had no clue what they were talking about, but Reuben, one of the organizers, turned to me and said, "Don't be confused. I will explain everything."

The hour-long meeting was interesting. Everyone had a different accent, and they were all different shapes, sizes, and colors. There were no feelings of arrogance or pompousness traveling around the room; just a group of simple people who were there to serve a bigger purpose. There was an energy of love and mutual respect.

When the board filled up, people began dragging luggage into their cars. A few said goodbye and disappeared while Reuben, three other people, and I stayed in the warehouse.

Reuben took me aside and explained that there were three different aspects to the work they did. The first was the warehouse, where all the containers came from. The clothes were organized and put in boxes according to the item, age, and gender.

There was also a pile of "inappropriate clothes" that would go to the locals. I chuckled, but Reuben didn't seem to find that funny.

"What do you mean by inappropriate?" I asked.

In his thick, Swiss accent, he said, "Well, clothes that we think are torn, dirty, or would be disrespectful to their culture. The locals can take them for free."

The volunteers had two shifts in the warehouse. One was from 9:00 a.m. to 2:00 p.m. and the second was from 2:00 p.m. to 7:00 p.m. He said most people did double shifts and stayed there the whole day.

The second aspect of the work was the Children's Home—a place in downtown Chios where refugees from the camp could shower and pick up diapers and sanitary pads. There was even a space filled with toys for their children to play in. Reuben drove me there, and we parked in the city and walked about a mile into a bazaar. Next to a shop that was selling fresh fish was a door. Reuben knocked. I recognized the girl who opened the door from the morning meeting. There was a set of stairs going up. I walked behind the two of them, and when we reached the top, it was a sight I would never forget. There were about four rooms; one was a walk-in closet and had one volunteer and two refugee families choosing clothes. A little boy around three or four came running to show us his "new" jacket with Mowgli from *The Jungle Book* on it.

The second room was attached to the bathroom, so people could shower and then come out to use deodorant, body lotion, and a hairdryer. A volunteer waited in that room and helped distribute supplies. I saw an older girl who was around ten years old dry her younger sister's hair. They were giggling. When I asked what was going on, the older one pointed at her hair and—in an Arabic accent—said, "Soft and nice."

The third and fourth rooms were filled with toys and books for children of all ages, from infants to preteens who enjoyed playing, coloring, or drawing. The parents sat at the side watching their children just be children. The walls were decorated with pictures and paintings. There was another tiny area with boxes of juice, fruit, and chips handed out by volunteers to the families as they left. The volunteers also worked two shifts here. And after the Children's House would close at 5:00 p.m., the volunteers would disinfect every toy, sweep, clean the bathroom, wash the towels, and clean the entire place.

The third aspect of the volunteer work was the most difficult. When there was news of a boat arriving, the volunteers on-call would run to the coast and wait behind the police. Once the police had registered everyone, the volunteers would take them into portable rooms. In the rooms, the refugees received warm clothes, shoes, tea, food, and blankets. From there, they were transported to the camps.

Reuben took me to the shore where landings happened, showed me the rooms, and registered me with the Chios police.

I had a chance to interview Reuben that day:

Tell me a little bit about yourself.

Hi, my name is Ruben and I am from Belgium. Back home, I am a construction worker and an electrician. I volunteer with a few different organizations, mostly for locals that are going through a difficult time. I love sports, especially volleyball and gardening.

If you could use one word to describe yourself, what would it be?

The one word I would like to use for myself is "storm." Another volunteer by the name of Tess did a Mayan reading for me and told me I was a resonant storm, which means I have a lot of energy and do everything with a lot of passion. I feel this is true, and I keep pushing myself to the brink of exhaustion, and then I stop.

Why did you decide to volunteer with CESRT - Chios Eastern Shore Response Team?

I have always volunteered in my community. In Belgium, we have a large number of Syrian and Iraqi refugees, and so I have some experience working with them. Some of my friends who had volunteered in Chios told me about the situation here. Listening to what they said made me angry that not enough people were helping in this crisis, and so I decided to come here and volunteer. I connected with CESRT through my friends. I had decided to take one year off work and figure out what to do next. My work wasn't fulfilling, and I felt like I was losing my spirit. So, after much thought, I decided to take a year off and travel around Europe. But after hearing about the stories here, I decided to postpone my travels and offer help in a place that urgently needed it.

Why couldn't you do the same work at home? Why come so far?

I felt that the refugees in Belgium were still in a better situation than they are here in Chios. People arrive here and don't know what will happen. They leave everything behind and come to an unknown future, and I feel like people here need more help.

What have you learned about the refugee situation that you didn't know before?

Before coming here, I knew nothing about the refugee crisis on this island. But after working here, I learned the reasons why people leave everything behind. I heard their stories and created friendships.

Another eye-opener was the way the camps are run. I believed that big organizations were doing a wonderful job, but after seeing it firsthand, I noticed the lack of communication and how unorganized the whole system is. I think if all the organizations that are working to help the refugees worked together and communicated well, we could achieve so much more.

How was your experience at the Vial Camp?

My first experience at the Vial camp was great as we got to play games with the kids. We organized lots of games so the children could have some fun and the parents could get a break from childcare. It was a wonderful experience. We weren't allowed to go inside the camp, so we played outdoor games. The most shocking experience was when there was a storm and the tents caved in. The police made the refugees wait three to four hours in the rain before they were able to fix the situation. People were shivering and waiting in the storm while all their belongings got soaked.

What is your fondest memory of volunteering in Chios?

My fondest memory was during a landing. A man got off the boat and was so happy. He opened his phone and started to take selfies with everyone. He knew one word of English which was "selfie." Even now when I meet him, he is always smiling, and his positive energy is contagious. From far away, we see each other and call out "selfie" to each other, and it makes us both smile.

How do you plan to raise awareness in your community about the refugee crisis?

When I go back home, I want to start a project about people who are being trafficked. This is a project that is already taking place in Switzerland. It allows people to understand what refugees go through when they are trafficked in the middle of the night and locked in rooms with many people. I would love to start a project like that in Belgium. I also want to talk to university students who are in their last year about coming here to volunteer—especially social workers who can and gain knowledge and experience while doing something good for others.

What is your message to the world?

My message to the world is that being aware is the most important thing. In Belgium, the news channels will sugarcoat what is happening. I believe that if there is shocking news, it should be shown as shocking because if people aren't aware of a problem, how can they help? I also wish that I could one day erase racism and let people understand that we are all one and should live in harmony and peace.

***

I encountered many refugees during my time as a volunteer. While going to the Children's Home in downtown Chios, I saw a young man with long hair skateboarding. Every time he saw me and the other volunteers, he came by with a big smile and a warm hello. When I asked another volunteer who he was, she told me he was a young refugee living alone in Chios. I asked if I could interview him, and she connected us. Here is his story:

Do you live alone here?

Yes, but now the people in the camps have become my family. I used to live there, but since Souda camp shut down, I am living with two of my cousins in an apartment.

How did you get here?

I left my home in Syria when I was fourteen years old. When we fled Syria, my family was given asylum in Germany, but my case was denied even though I was a minor at that time. My family, which included my parents and two brothers, left Syria for Turkey while they waited for my papers to be approved. My parents eventually sent my two brothers to Germany so they could start school, and they waited for me in Istanbul, Turkey. I had already arrived in Turkey but was hiding in a city called Adana. The goal was to get to Istanbul without getting caught and from there go to Chios, Greece. Once in Greece, I could apply for my asylum again and then reunite with my family in Germany. My father asked me if I wanted to try to get to Germany illegally and deal with the consequences later. I told him I didn't want to go like that; we had heard stories of people being arrested, and then they just vanished shortly after. My father gave me two options— either the whole family stays back in Turkey and revokes their asylee visa to Germany, or I take the long route and go through a human smuggler who could get me to my destination. I decided to go with the human smuggler.

That must've been a difficult decision.

It was, but I also didn't want to put my whole family's future in jeopardy.

What happened next?

The smugglers picked me up and took me to a hotel. I had some cash that my father sent, a few pieces of clothes, and a cell phone. I stayed in the hotel all alone for about two weeks. They told me to wait there while they organized everything, and so I quietly went outside to get some food and then waited all alone in the old hotel. Finally, one night, I heard loud banging on the door. They gave me my passport, told me to get my things and meet them outside. I picked up my belongings and ran out to where I saw a small truck. They motioned for me to climb into the back and close the door. It was dark, and after riding for a short while, they stopped, opened the back door, and motioned for more people to enter the back. This happened a few times. It started to get crowded inside. Finally, the truck stopped, but the door didn't open for a long time. My heart sank as I knew we had reached wherever we were supposed to go. Eventually, the door opened, and one of the smugglers ushered everyone out. I was one of the last people off the truck. When I looked up, I could only see a few stars in the sky, and as my feet touched the ground, I could feel the wet mud beneath them. I stood with another family whose little girl started to cry. Seeing that the mother was holding another baby, I picked up the crying girl. The smuggler told us angrily to keep our voices down, our phones off, and to follow him. And so, we followed the sounds of his feet walking through the mud.

How many people were with you?

I was able to roughly count the people, and from what I could see, there were seventeen of us. We walked for hours until the sun started to rise, and we finally saw a river and a boat in front of us. The smuggler told us to get in, but it was small and broken, and we all refused. He argued with us, but we collectively decided not to get in. He grew frustrated and told us to hide under the tree until he returned. We hid under different trees and waited. It started to drizzle, and we waited in the rain for what seemed like a very long time. That was the moment when I felt scared and thought I was going to die. He finally came back a few hours later with another boat. We quietly got in and crossed the river. He ordered us to get off.

It was early morning at that point and there was only a little bit of light. The smuggler gave us a map, told us where we were and pointed toward the route we had to take to reach our destination. Some of the other people started to ask him questions, but before he could answer us, he ran back to the boat and sailed away. We decided to hide in the bushes until it was nighttime again. Once it got very dark, two other families and I started walking. We heard dogs barking in the distance and voices coming closer and closer. We tried to hide, but pretty soon, the dogs and the Turkish police were right next to us. They arrested us, put us in a car, and drove off. No one had any idea where we were going. I knew a little bit of Turkish and tried to reason with the officers, but they hit me and told me to be quiet. We arrived at the police station, and they motioned us to go inside. Then. they forced us to the back of the building and put us in a prison with about forty other people. They put the women and children in the same room, and we told them to separate us, but we were yelled at and beaten, again.

Did you want to cry? I can't even imagine how you felt as a child.

I think. I was so sure we would be killed that I was numb. I really didn't feel like a child; just like humans fighting for survival. Around 7:00 a.m., the police came in and took us all out. The men were put in one truck, and I was put with the women and children in the other. We headed toward the refugee camps in Turkey, from there to Chios, and eventually to Germany.

Tell me about your life now.

I am nineteen years old and still here in Chios. It's been five years since I left my home country for a better future. I look so different from how I did when my family last saw me. I am so much taller, and my hair is so long. My mother was shocked when she saw a video of me. I try to remain positive, but some days it's really difficult. I miss my family terribly and hope to be reunited soon. I spend my days rollerblading, and I have also learned how to play the guitar on my own.

***

This story is similar to that of hundreds of thousands of Syrian families who fled the war. The Syrian conflict began in March 2011 when a group of teenagers in the city of Derra were arrested and tortured for painting pro-democracy slogans on the school walls. This ignited a series of protests all over the country. The security forces had orders to shut down any protests and open fire wherever an anti-government demonstration took place. Many people were killed, and instead of silencing the protestors, their voices only grew louder. By July 2011, thousands of people flooded the streets protesting and demanding President Bashar Al Asad's resignation. The security forces killed several protestors, which caused anti-government groups to take up arms against the security forces. The tension and violence only increased as rebel groups and militia were formed to take over cities and towns. By April 2012, about a year after the initial conflict, the fighting had reached Damascus—the capital of Syria—and the major city of Aleppo. According to the UN, by June 2013, an estimated 90,000 people had been killed as the country plummeted into a full-blown civil war. The number of casualties kept increasing, and four years later in 2015, the death toll had reached over 250.000.

Today, the civil war is about much more than just anti-government protests and has deepened its cause and planted its roots in many different ways. Now, aside from government forces fighting the "rebels," it has also become a sectarian conflict—with the Sunni Muslims fighting against the Shia Muslims along with the rise of ISIS—the violent *jihadist* group that has caused havoc in the lives of Syrian civilians.

According to a UN Commission of Inquiry, all sides in the war have committed human rights violations and war crimes that include murder, torture, rape, kidnapping, and disappearances, as well as blocking the entrance of food, water, and health services to civilians. In August of 2013, hundreds of people in Damascus were killed by rockets filled with sarin, a highly toxic nerve agent. All parties involved in the conflict denied using the chemical weapon; nevertheless, western powers have blamed it on the Syrian government. Even though President Assad promised the complete removal of chemical weapons, the Organization for the Prohibition of Chemical Weapons (OPCW) has continued to find the use of toxic chemical weapons in the conflict.

The war is now in its eighth year, causing a huge humanitarian crisis that has impacted the whole world. According to Al-Jazeera, an Arabic-language television channel from Doha, Qatar, more than 465,000 Syrians have been killed in the fighting, over a million injured, and over 12 million—half the country's pre-war population—have been displaced from their homes.

Many of these refugees leave through human smugglers. Their ultimate goal is often to obtain asylum in any European country that will take them. There are two ways the smugglers bring people to Turkey and Greece, where they have to wait to apply for asylum. The first is by land and sea, but the journey can be long and arduous, especially during the cold winters. They must wait for days before the smugglers find enough people to fill the boats. The other way is to seek a fake passport. The smugglers create fake passports by using stolen documents—a kind of identity theft.

They prefer passports from Italy, Spain, Albania, Bulgaria, and France because it is easier for light-skinned Syrians to pass as residents of these countries. Photo-similar passports are the ones in which the picture of the original passport holder resembles the refugee. This allows them to take on a new identity with a lower chance of being caught. The other way of making a fake passport is when smugglers carefully rip out the page with the picture on it and add a new one or leave the page in and add a new picture on top. This is called a photo-change passport and requires a great deal of practice to be done correctly and masterfully. Many of those who offer photo-change passport services use CorelDRAW, a graphic design tool.

Getting a fake passport is much more expensive than traveling by land and sea, so most refugees travel without passports. They spend days and weeks alone in the cold of winter until the smugglers are able to find a way to take them to their destination. Sometimes. they are put on boats and told to go in a certain direction. They are told someone will be available at the other end to get them. Unknowingly, these refugees are sold fake life vests made of plastic and the boats they are put on are old and damaged. The boats are little dinghies—small rubber boats with a mast and sails. In the western world, a dinghy is used mostly for recreational purposes and racing. A smuggler's boat that comfortably holds a maximum of fifteen people often carries forty-five to fifty people in one trip. Not only that, but smugglers can also charge up to $3500 for smuggling one person. They are usually paid 30% before the journey starts, and once the refugee reaches the promised destination, the remaining 70% is paid in cash. If for any reason, they can't pay the remaining amount, they are beaten, raped, and tortured. Some of the refugee women and children are sold to brothels and traffickers to recover the money from the family. If a family member dies enroute, the smugglers will not return the money to the families. These terms are usually discussed verbally before the journey begins.

I spoke to a trafficker on the phone. His voice was soft, and he spoke slowly as if he were choosing his words carefully. Our conversation went as follows:

Tell me about yourself.

My name is Rashad. I am from Iraq and now live in Turkey. My country was severely bombed, and most of my family was killed. I lived with my wife, son, and parents. My wife and father were killed in the bombing, and my son, who was fourteen, was kidnapped.

How was he kidnapped?

I honestly don't know what happened. I had taken my mother to the village to meet her family. When I came back, everything was ruined. My home was gone; all that remained were crushed concrete and bricks. Where I had a happy life full of laughter, now there was only silence or the sounds of bombs and people wailing. The neighbors said, "They have taken your son." I don't know who "they" were. I hope and pray every day that I find him. And so, my mother and I came to Turkey.

How did you feel when you left?

I was devastated when I left. That was my home and my everything. Everything was taken away, and I was like an empty carcass, trying to stay alive for the sake of my mother. Coming to Turkey made me realize that many like me were running away from the war and destruction. I wanted to help so badly but didn't know what to do. I worked in a factory and through other refugees, met Jon.

Who is Jon?

Jon was the most prominent human trafficker in the area. But he didn't call himself that; he called himself the "people mover." He believed he moved people from agony to a good life. Jon always said that if one family member had to suffer or die on the way, at least the rest were saved. He was a big, old man who spoke seven or eight different languages. He had about ten agents working under him. He asked if I wanted to help and make money along the way. I needed the money and thought I could help people.

Did you understand the exact nature of the work?

At that time, I believed I was helping people. When I started, I was given a list of people, and I had to walk with them to the coast in the middle of the night where I handed them over to another man who took them across on a boat.

When did you realize it was dangerous work?

On my second trip, there was a family who had a tiny newborn baby. The baby was very sick and died in the night from malnutrition. The mother tried so hard not to make noise while crying, but she did. I had to leave the young parents and move ahead because I didn't want to get the other twenty-three people caught by the police. Finally, they found us, and when I asked about the baby, they told me they had buried her. Later, I found out from the man who took them on the boat that the mother jumped in the sea and had died as well. That was very difficult for me, and I was traumatized for days after, but we are humans, and slowly, I forgot the pain of that mother and continued my work.

How do you feel about the work now?

It has been four years since I started this work, and I feel nothing. I now do more complicated things like making fake passports or ID cards to show that the refugees are legal residents.

Do you feel any guilt?

People usually see human traffickers as evil. I honestly don't feel much guilt anymore. Yes, I am human, but people always think I don't have a heart. Remember, I need to feed my family. I got married again and have twin girls. This work pays well, and if out of one hundred people, I help fifty start a new life, I think that isn't bad. How many people out there preach about religion and engage in charity work that helps that many people? They only preach; we help people start new lives. I am so glad my mother never found out about this. She died two years ago. I know she would have tried to discourage me.

***

Many volunteers come from all over the world to help refugees. I was lucky enough to work with them side-by-side. During my time volunteering, I shadowed a few of my peers because I wanted to know what made them leave their families. Each and every one of them was always smiling despite the tough circumstances. I was there only for a little while, and I felt terrible about the situation. I believed that it took a lot more than being human to stay and help people in the camps for months at a time. I still believe this. Yet, there were so many of them who engaged in this type of work, and who did so happily. These Rescue Team workers were and still are my heroes.

One day, as we worked in the warehouse, a tall man with curly hair walked in. There was something about him that caught my eye; he looked kind and sweet. He was tall and muscular. He seemed to have a rough and tough exterior, but his eyes spoke the language of compassion. We were told he was the new volunteer and he had been working with rescue teams. He helped with the building materials and other labor-induced work and luckily, I had a chance to talk to him about this:

Tell me about yourself.

I used to be a TV producer and had a perfect life. In 2015, I watched the news about the refugee crisis, and it broke something inside of me. I was always able to explain what was happening to my children, but when I saw the image of the little Syrian boy whose body washed up on the beach in Turkey, I couldn't explain that.

How did you get involved with refugees?

I quit my job and went to join a rescue team on the island of Lesbos, Greece. The first time we went out to rescue someone was when we got news of a plastic boat stuck in the middle of the sea. When we got there, among the other refugees was an elderly Yazidi woman who had about ten to twelve children clinging to her. When I looked into the children's eyes, I saw an emptiness that was filled with fear. I know that sounds contradictory, but that is what I saw. It was like they were waiting for another encounter with the "enemy." The emptiness was a lack of hope, and the fear came from the unfamiliar. I learned that later as I went out on more rescues. Many children don't believe we are here to help when they first see us. Their faith in humanity has been damaged and they can't understand why we would want to help.

What is one rescue that stays with you?

Another rescue that I clearly remember happened on October 3rd, 2016. We were in the Central Mediterranean, twenty miles north of the Libyan coast in international waters. We had been at sea for two weeks having technical issues with the boat, and there was a storm coming. We knew that sooner or later; the boats would be coming. I remember being in my bed at 3:00 a.m. when the alarm went off. In five minutes, we were moving towards five to six boats filled with refugees. We worked for twenty hours and rescued six hundred people that day; fifty died. It was one of the most traumatic yet also the most rewarding rescue mission.

It was pitch dark and the sea was very rough. We were getting close to a rubber boat containing one hundred and fifty people. During a rescue mission, we approached the boat from the back because if we were on the side, the boat would be at risk of tipping over. So, as we aligned our boat with the dinghy, we began asking people not to hand us their luggage because we needed to save lives first. As you can imagine, it was a chaotic situation. People were screaming and pushing each other; everyone was wearing life jackets, and no one could swim. The boat had a tiny hole in it causing seawater to mix with urine and petrol, so there was an awful smell. People were pushing each other, and as one person fell, the others trampled over them. Mothers and fathers tried to keep their children safe and held their hands. Grandmothers tried to keep their balance while the young pushed them to the side. It was a horrific scene.

There was a storm in the sky and in the water, but what we saw in front of us was the war between life and death. These people gave up so much for the desire to live a better life. The first thing we asked was if there were any children, babies, pregnant women, or elderly. We wore a little band on our head that held a red flashlight (as white lights tend to be blinding) and through that tiny beam of red light, I saw hands go up and a package being passed through them. I was irritated. "Why are you giving me your luggage?" I yelled out loud. No one paid attention, and they finally handed it to me. With extreme frustration, I grabbed the package, looked into it, and I saw a tiny little African face. It was a beautiful child wrapped in a wet, dirty piece of cloth, asleep and oblivious of the chaos around it. I stopped and began to weep. It felt like God was showing me that there is always hope, even in the most desperate situations. It was an incredible moment amid all that chaos.

I met the mother a few days later at the camp and realized it was a four-day-old baby. She hugged me and we both cried. I hope this child will never remember the first few days of her life.

***

After chatting with Rob, I wanted to talk to others. Instead of doing the volunteer work that I was there to do, I began focusing more on the rescue team workers and choosing the ones I wanted to talk to. One young man stood out. He was my son's age. He was both energetic and knowledgeable about the crisis. It was incredible and very impressive.

A volunteer introduced me to Leo as one of the administrators. He was a young man and had bright blond hair and a full beard. Leo was one of the volunteers who had a lot of data about the refugee situation and was also interested in the political aspects of it. Below is my conversation with him:

Tell me about yourself.

I am Leonardo Sandrinelli, twenty-six years old, from the

Italian part of Switzerland. I got involved with refugees after I finished high school. I went to the French part of Switzerland for university and got a degree in social science and social politics. After I graduated, I went to Australia for a year to improve my English.

How did you start working with refugees?

When I came back home, I worked with refugees for the Swiss government. My job focused mostly on administrative work where refugees and asylum seekers came to us for doctor's appointments or monthly payments, and we would give out the information they were looking for. Then, I decided to pursue a master's in social sciences with a specialization in migration and citizenship. While getting my degree, I worked again in a residential program for asylum seekers with mostly men and a handful of women. At the university, I also taught French classes to refugees to help with their resettlement.

I decided to do my thesis on the role of technology in the lives of refugees—how they were using it to plan the trip, during the trip, and once they got in Switzerland. I worked with a group of Afghan refugees in their twenties. There was one young man who spoke a bit of French and he helped me translate. I learned that the cell phone was very useful for their journey.

A lot of your work and degree revolved around working with refugees. Was it a conscious decision or was it something that just fell in your lap, and you decided to pursue it?

I come from a social worker family; my mother started an organization working with local children, and my father was also a social assistant and worked with families. Growing up, I always saw my parents helping others and so they built that foundation in me. Working with refugees, I was able to see their struggle firsthand. I also love to travel and learn about other cultures, so I think that also helped me with my decision. The refugee crisis was getting bigger and bigger and when I was twenty-one, I started to get involved and decided to work with them. Last year, I got involved in a Swiss Italian organization, and I worked in Thessaloniki.

What are your future plans?

I would like to continue and spend my time working with refugees. The right-wing conservatives are getting more powerful all over the world, and they mainly say no to refugees. We, as a society, are lacking in resettlement programs for these people. They get asylum but struggle with many things like language and creating a community. I would like to start a community center and a radio project and teach them vocational skills so they can take care of themselves and their families. When people are traumatized from war, and they are not given the skills to survive. It creates a sense of helplessness.

What is the one thing you learned during your work?

The most important thing I learned during my experience and my work with refugees is the nonverbal language of humanity. Without speaking the same language, you can have a full conversation with any human being. You can do this by showing that you care, using hand gestures, and being a friend. I know I can communicate with anyone using this nonverbal language of humanity.

Tell me a little more about your experiences?

One Afghan refugee I worked with in Switzerland was nineteen. His family was stuck in Greece, and his father had passed away. His mother was there with four other children but because he was nineteen, he couldn't sponsor his family. So, they had to wait. They didn't know when their paperwork would be processed, or whether they would be approved or rejected. The only good thing about this is that I was able to get the money from the young boy and take it to his mother in Greece. It's been two years, and they are now in Serbia— still waiting. When giving asylum to refugees, the governments usually prioritize pregnant women, the elderly, disabled people, and children. Men are always forgotten or last on the list. If you are seventeen, you are considered a minor, but once you turn eighteen, you become part of the forgotten ones. Some of the men in the camps have been there for a very long time, waiting to be reunited with their families.

How do you think the situation will improve?

Firstly, I believe that the situation is created not because of economic reasons; it's all about politics. They always talk about the crisis being too big to handle, but the truth is that Europe has a lot of money. It's not a real crisis because of the numbers; it's more about how they are being managed. Europe has a population of 550 million while they have been only one million refugees. Migration has always existed along with human history. It's all about big politicians and big corporations.

What is your fondest memory of the work you're doing?

My fondest memory of the camps is when I was working in Thessaloniki. A girl with autism in a family of ten was screaming all night long and wasn't letting anyone else sleep. I brought her music to calm her down, and it was soothing for her. I really connected with that family, and now they are in France. I have a before and after picture of the girl; she is so much happier. I also love the gratitude these people have no matter what you do. As long as you show up and greet them, they welcome you. One time, I wanted to get some milk for a family, and when I got back from the market, I found a huge table of food prepared for me. I started crying. They didn't have their own food but prepared a feast for me.

What is one word that describes you?

If I had to describe myself in one word, it would be "compassionate" because I always put myself in other people's shoes before I speak and act.

***

Another volunteer I talked to was Janne. She was a strikingly beautiful woman from Norway. Every time I needed help, I asked her; she was always there for me. She is a mother, volunteer, and business owner.

Tell me about yourself.

My name is Janne, pronounced "Yana," and I am from Norway. My husband and I have four adult children and own a company.

Why did you choose this cause?

When I first heard about the refugee situation in spring 2015, I was really upset and wanted to help. My children were all grown up and had moved away, so I had the freedom to do whatever was needed. I contacted a few organizations like UNHCR and asked them how I could help. The work they had was mostly administrative office work, but I wanted to actively help at the front lines. In January of 2016, I left Norway, came to Greece, and became the coordinator of a wonderful Norwegian organization called A Drop in the Ocean. I stayed there for about ten months. I learned so much while working with this organization. I worked in the camps, distributed food and clothes, and got to witness the refugee situation firsthand.

Why volunteer with CESRT (Chios Eastern Shore Response Team)?

After working there for some time, I felt like there was a huge need for a place where children could be children. I felt like they were not given the opportunity to have a normal, healthy childhood. One thing that was alarming to me was that the kids didn't cry if they got hurt. I felt like it could be because they had either gotten used to the pain, or they felt like no one cared because their parents were dealing with so much trauma on their own. Being a preschool teacher, I really saw the need to create a children's center where kids could play, and parents could just be parents. I started to work with an organization from Switzerland and asked them if they felt there was a need for a children's house, and they said yes. I also asked the refugee mothers what they thought of it, and they totally agreed—it was a great idea! All the work and planning for the Children's House was done with the help of refugee mothers. But we needed someone who understood the language, and so I contacted a local organization and asked them what they thought about the idea for the Children's House. They loved the idea, and we all worked together and opened the Children's House *on January 2nd, 2017.*

If you could use one word to describe yourself, what would it be?

One word would be "mother" because I feel motherly towards people and worry about their wellbeing. I try to take care of the people around me.

What have you learned about the refugee situation that you didn't know before?

Before working with the refugees, they seemed like they were unreal—something distant. But once I started working with them, I realized there wasn't much difference between us; little Noora and Muhammed were just like my children. I got to meet Maria from Syria who was a medical student and had to leave because of the bombings in her city. Like me, she had dreams and hopes for the future. It also made me realize that when someone leaves everything they'd ever owned behind for the safety of their family, they must have endured awful things in their own country. They leave their entire universe behind and get on small boats with nothing; some parents send their children alone because they fear for their safety. I feel so blessed that just because I was born in Norway, my fate is different from these families. My heart breaks for them.

How do you plan to raise awareness in your community about the refugee crisis?

It makes me sad that we have so much space and money in Norway to take care of these families, yet the government has decided that there is no crisis. But I try my best to share the news and images on Facebook. I talk to my friends and family, and with the help of a Norwegian organization, I have raised 1500 euros.

What is your message to the world?

I believe we are all one, and we need to start taking care of each other and this beautiful little planet that we live on.

***

Refugees continue to arrive on the island of Chios, Greece because once they are on the islands of Chios or Lesbos, they can apply to relocate to Athens. Once the refugees arrive on the island, the police give them an ID card. They then reside either in the camps or rent an apartment together with other refugee families. The government of Greece gives them ninety euros per month, which is very little compared to their expenses. So many of them search for employment at restaurants or stores in hopes of making more money to cover the costs of living. They submit their paperwork and undergo a seven to eight-hour interview that grants them permission to go to Athens. Once in Athens, they can start the application process for asylum. At first, the camps were created for the refugees to stay for only two to three weeks, but today, some of them have been stuck there for years.

The tiny island of Chios has been impacted by the influx of refugees. Some locals have extremely negative feelings toward them, while others, like my friend, Pothiti, try their best to help the situation. She is the founder of the Chios Eastern Shore Response Team. Below is a snippet of her story:

The refugees had been arriving in Chios since July of 2015, but I had never witnessed a landing on the beach next to my home. I remember that day very clearly. About two and a half years ago, in the early morning hours, I woke up to the sound of crying and screaming. I ran to my balcony but couldn't see anything, so I left my son sleeping at home and ran to the beach where the sounds were coming from. What I saw there was horrible: forty to fifty refugees were coming off a boat in freezing weather, soaking wet, crying, and scared. I felt helpless because so many children looked terrified. But I did what I could and took them to three rooms in my motel so they could warm up and feel better. That was the beginning of everything. It changed me as a person. It's sad but true that as humans, we don't understand how awful a situation is until we see it with our own two eyes. It was also the beginning of an initiative to help them. Today, CESRT is a group of dedicated volunteers from all over the world. In two years, 2000 registered volunteers have passed through here to help refugees. That day, I started to wonder how any mother could put her child on a plastic boat that was so dangerous and let her child go. But I realized that they didn't have an option; the danger in their home was larger than the danger at sea or in the hands of a human smuggler. I started to see these mothers and fathers as heroes because they were just trying to keep their families alive.

Part Three

Bangladesh

Bangladesh has always been on my list of destinations that I wanted to visit. When I started this journey, Bangladesh appeared on my radar. I wanted to talk to the Rohingya Muslim refugees living in camps there.

The Rohingya are a Muslim minority who derive their religious beliefs from Sufism under the Suni Muslim sect. Currently, there are around 3.5 million Rohingya Muslims worldwide. However, before 2017, around one million of them lived in Myanmar's Rakhine State. Myanmar (formerly known as Burma) is home to over one hundred different ethnic and religious groups, yet the dominant religion is Buddhism.

Since Myanmar's independence in 1948, most ruling parties have rejected the Rohingya's historical claims and refuse to recognize the group as the country's official ethnic group. They are termed as being "illegal immigrants" that have come from Bangladesh. Additionally, Bangladesh used to be East Pakistan before the war in 1971, when it became an independent sovereign nation.

Growing up, I remember my mother describing that war and how they cried when a part of Pakistan was taken away from them. My parents were visiting West Pakistan—as it was called at the time—when I was about six-months-old. The war broke out and my parents ended up staying there for a few months until it was safe to leave as air travel was limited during the war. My mother told us how they had a kinship and special bond with the people of East Pakistan—now known as Bangladesh. I always had a desire to visit Bangladesh since it was part of my ancestry, but in so many ways, it also wasn't.

And so, I planned to go to Bangladesh the first week of January 2019.

I had already contacted an organization that works in the camps on the border between Bangladesh and Myanmar. They told me very clearly not to mention to anyone that I was coming to talk to the refugees.

In October 2018, I received my funding, and in November, I went to the Bangladeshi embassy to obtain a visa. I was told that I should get the visa at the airport and that it shouldn't be an issue at all. The guy waved my blue American passport in the air and said, "You have this! Nothing to worry about! Just get your ticket and they will give you your visa at the airport. Blue passport is always good to have." He smiled.

I got back home and a few of my Bangladeshi friends told me that it would be much better if I had a visa stamped on my passport before I landed in Dhaka.

So, once again, I took the day off and braved the traffic from Orange County to Los Angeles. I walked in and was hoping not to see the same guy as I was worried he would repeat the same instructions he did earlier.

I walked in confidently, tried to do something different with my hair, and put on a different outfit. As I entered the consulate, I saw the same guy sitting behind the counter. I sighed and stood in line. About five people stood in front of me. When my turn came, I walked straight up to him because he was the only one at the front desk and said, "Good morning."

"Hello, *baji* (older sister). How can I help you?" Thankfully, he didn't seem to remember me.

I went on to tell him that I needed a visa for Bangladesh,

and he told me that because there were elections going on in Bangladesh, it could take from six to eight weeks. Even after that, it could be denied. He said the same thing again—that I could just go to the airport and try to get a visa there. He was confident I would get it. But then with a slight giggle, he said, "If they deny you at the airport, you could just always come back. Or go somewhere else."

"That is such a waste of money!" I exclaimed at the horror of his giggling.

Then, he flipped through my passport and asked, "You're from Pakistan?" He frowned.

"No, I'm American."

"But in your passport, you have many entry stamps to Pakistan. You go to Pakistan many times?"

"Yes, my parents live there."

He quietly shook his head. Even though his mouth curved into a semi-smile, the frown lines on his forehead deepened. He handed me my passport and said goodbye.

"What should I do about my visa?" I insisted.

"Sister, you will not get it from here. If you really want to go there, just go and get it from the airport. I can't help you."

The family behind me pushed me aside and moved toward the counter as he motioned for the next in line. I quietly put my passport back into the big, manilla envelope that held all my important papers and slowly walked towards the exit.

I left feeling much more confused and upset and didn't know what to do. I was still curious and wanted to interview more refugees. I also wanted to talk to more people involved in the crisis. I was so sure that the only place to go was Bangladesh that I started to feel like my whole project was on the verge of collapsing should I be denied entry.

As I was discussing my dilemma with a friend, he asked me, "Why don't you go to Nepal instead?"

"Nepal?"

"Yeah, don't you know that Nepal has a large number of refugees from Tibet and Bhutan?"

I did know that, but for some reason, my fascination with Bangladesh made me forget it. My heart started to race. "But it's already November; how am I supposed to find an organization to work with? Or that would help me to get in touch with refugees?"

"Stop making excuses, Tami. If this is something you really want to do, then go for it. It's a beautiful country. You will love it."

My friend is a schoolteacher and has worked locally and internationally with refugees as well. He had some contacts in Nepal and sent out a few emails to get me in touch with the necessary people there who could help me move my project forward. Within a day, he received a response. He connected me with a young man named Santosh Shah. Santosh is the president of the Leadership Academy in Nepal that encourages and trains young people to take on leadership roles.

I asked him if they could set up interviews so that I could understand where Nepal stands in terms of the resettlement and betterment of the refugees. Within a week, Santosh had emailed me an itinerary and a plan to meet refugees in the area.

And just like that, I was going to Nepal!

What an incredible opportunity life had given me. The country had been on my vision board for the past three years. I have a few friends from Nepal, and they often talk about the beauty and hospitality of that small piece of land. So, when this opportunity fell in my lap, I was thrilled. I couldn't believe how the universe had worked in my favor to take me to my dream place where I could interview refugees.

Part Four

Nepal

I was set to leave for Nepal on January 1ˢᵗ, 2019. It was a long flight from Los Angeles and once I got there, Santosh and his team assured me that they would take care of everything. I got to the airport and as I got out, I saw a young lady by the name of Alisha with a card that had my name on it. We exchanged messages before, so she knew what I looked like, and I knew what she looked like. We hugged and then she led me to a car waiting to take me to the hotel. On the way, she told me that the hotel we were going to was owned by a Tibetan refugee and her parents. My excitement was overflowing; I couldn't believe that I was in Nepal for the next ten days.

***

The history of Tibet is rich and full of religious, political, and cultural upheavals. In 1935, the young man to become the fourteenth Dalai Lama was born in a small village in Tibet. In 1937, he was declared by Buddhist officials to be the reincarnation of the past thirteen Dalai Lamas. In 1950, the Dalai Lama was officially made the head of state of Tibet. In 1951, China enforced an agreement with Tibetan leaders known as the "17 Point Agreement." This agreement allowed Chinese civil and military headquarters in Tibet. It was also supposed to give Tibetans the freedom to practice their own religion. The Chinese army destroyed many monasteries and killed thousands of people. The tension between Tibetans and the Chinese increased, thus causing civilian protests to erupt across the country, and the tension began to rise. In 1959, the Dalai Lama was forced to flee to India and was followed by 80,000 of his people. The Dalai Lama then took asylum in Dharamsala in Northern India.

Around 20,000 of His Holiness's followers took refuge in Nepal. Some of them lived in camps that have now become settlements.

***

A couple of days after, I arrived in Kathmandu. I flew to the city of Pokhara, which is considered one of the most beautiful places in Nepal. It is the second-largest city, and it's surrounded by mountains with Phewa Lake at its center. The local airline of Nepal is called Yeti Airlines, which made me chuckle.

When I arrived at the airport, I had planned to meet someone who would show me the city and take me to interview some refugees. He was a young man named Shreyaskar—another of Santosh's contacts.

Shreyaskar picked me up and we drove through the city, which was green with a backdrop of snowclad mountains. My hotel, Lakeview Resort, and Hotel was right across from Phewa Lake. The architecture of the hotel consisted of beautiful huts, and I was lucky enough to get one of the best rooms with a direct view of the lake. I arrived in the evening and decided to walk around the lake before dinner. Shreyaskar took me all around the lake and showed me the little gift shops. As we headed back to the hotel, we realized that there was a special sunset *puja* (prayer) going on. There were three priests who faced the declining sun and prayed. They sang hymns and used little lanterns to perform the *puja*.

Once I returned to the hotel, I watched a cultural show and dance and ate traditional food of the Himalayas people: lentil soup, rice, and vegetables.

The next morning, we drove to the camps in a van. During the drive, I noticed that the roads in Pokhara were much bigger and more open compared to those in Kathmandu. There was also less traffic and fewer people walking on the streets. We drove through main streets and reached an area with small houses connected to one another. We were told those were the camps that had become settlements; they had been there since the 1960s.

As we got out of our van, we saw a few men walking by. Our driver stopped in front of a man who sat on the steps in front of a house and asked him if he was willing to talk to us about his experience as a refugee. The man became a little uncomfortable and said we would have to talk to the head of the camp and get his permission before anyone else would talk to us. We asked a few other people who were wandering around. Two of them ignored us and one said the same thing. We asked where we would find the head of the camp, and a man pointed in a certain direction and said that he should be in the office over there. We walked that way toward a narrow, unpaved road, and suddenly, in the middle of these tiny broken houses, stood a majestic monastery with a huge, golden dome. It was one of the most beautiful monasteries I had ever seen. We continued to walk and finally found the office. Outside were four men standing and talking. My chaperone, Shreyaskar, asked them if they could talk to us or direct us toward someone who would be willing to be interviewed.

It seemed as though our request had upset the man that appeared to be the camp leader. He asked who we were and why we wanted to talk to refugees. The driver gently tried to tell him that I was a writer from America and wanted to interview refugees for a project I was working on.

He became uncomfortable and told us that they were too busy to help. He also said that we would have to go back and come another day and to ensure we make an appointment before we came next time.

I was leaving the next day. Shreyaskar suggested that we walk around again and try to find someone willing to talk to us.

We encountered a number of people, but still, no one agreed to talk to us.

We walked into a place where Tibetan women made carpets and sold them in the store next door. We saw an old man standing in front of the gate of someone's house while a dog was barking from inside. The man outside continued to talk to someone who was standing inside the gate. The dog barked, and the men continued to talk. As the man finished his conversation, he turned around and smiled at us. He was an older man in his sixties or seventies who had a big smile and walked with a cane. The driver asked if he would talk to us, and to our joy, the man agreed. Once he heard that I was from America, he started to speak to me in English.

He told us he didn't want to talk to us here as others might see him, and the camp head wouldn't like it. He said we could go to his store which was facing the main road. We quietly followed behind him to a little jewelry shop that had stunning silver items. He motioned for me to sit down, and we started to talk.

What is your name?

My name is Lhakba, which means Wednesday in Tibetan. I was born on—you guessed it right—a Wednesday, so my parents named me that.

When did you leave Tibet?

I left Tibet about forty years ago with a group of men. We were all around twelve or thirteen years old. When I fled, I left my whole family—my parents, my siblings, everyone—behind to join this caravan that was coming to Nepal.

Have you ever heard from your parents?

Someone that came from Tibet in 1975 told me that they were doing okay. After that, I have no idea if they are alive or dead. My father was sick in 1971.

Do you want to go back home to Tibet? Do you miss it?

Yes, I often think about going back, but we were told by our religious leader, His Holiness the Dalai Lama, to peacefully leave Tibet, and so we left. If I go back, I would be defying his orders, and also, we cannot live under China's communist regime.

You speak English very well. How did you learn?

Every time I talk to an American, they ask me the same question. I went to school for two years and learned the basics. I was always fascinated by the English language. I would look for pamphlets or brochures in English, take them out of the trashcan, and try to read them. I already knew the alphabet, and so I was always excited to learn about words. Once I was able to fully read a pamphlet in English, I bought a dictionary and started to look for new words to learn. After that, I would look in the dictionary and try to make sentences.

Tell me about your journey from Tibet?

Our journey was very difficult. We traveled on horses, and we stopped in the middle at small villages and exchanged our horses for food. It was a backbreaking journey, and many young boys died on the way. I was very lucky that I stayed alive. There were mountains, snow, rebel groups, slippery roads, thieves, and so many other factors. We didn't have proper clothes because they would get ripped during the journey. For food and water, priority was given to the old, sick, and younger ones.

We arrived in Nepal and stayed there for six to seven months. Then, a nonprofit organization helped us and sent us to India so that we could attend the Tibetan schools. I was fourteen at the time, but I had never been in school before. I had to start from kindergarten and did two grades in one year. After a year, I realized that I needed to earn some money, and so I enrolled in the Indian army and left school.

Did you enjoy being in the army?

It was okay. I fought in the 1971 war between Pakistan and India where we were able to free Bangladesh. I killed many Pakistanis. I also got trained to jump out of airplanes in the army. I planned to get more training so I could go back and fight for Tibet. I learned so many things. I learned some clerical office stuff too. I wanted to be the best for my country.

What else did you learn in the army?

I tried to learn many languages like Hindi, English, and even a little bit of French.

How did you like living in India? Why did you want to leave?

I loved India. Jawaharlal Nehru was a great man and helped Tibetans significantly. He gave us land, jobs, allowed us to join the Indian army, and even let us own businesses. But I wanted to go back home.

Why did you come back to Nepal?

I came to Nepal because I figured it was close to Tibet, and I could see my parents. It was only about ten cents to go there, but it was a lot more expensive from India.

What did you do when you first came here?

When I first came, we would get oranges from the farmers and sell them to the tourists that came to the city. Ever since then, I have lived in the settlement.

How long have these settlements been here?

They have been here since 1963. The settlements were made by the Red Cross but now, the government doesn't allow new people to come and live here. Only others like me who came in the 1960s can legally reside. I have to pay rent for my little house here which is 2000 rupees (around $100). But if some days I can't afford the rent, they are okay with it.

How would you describe life now?

Life is wonderful. I have three children and they are all doing well. I am not rich and can't give them gold or diamonds, but I did give them an education. My son is learning to be a physiotherapist, and one of my daughters works as a secretary. My wife is from Tibet also. She doesn't speak English though because she couldn't learn. She sells hand-woven baskets.

So, you lived in Tibet for twelve years of your life, and the rest of it you spent half in India and half in Nepal. Where is home?

I have been lucky that everywhere I went, I found good people that I can call family. Both India and Nepal have given me so much, but I think my heart will always be in Tibet.

But what really is home? Is it a building you live in or a place in your heart? I still don't know.

***

Bhutan is a small landlocked country that borders India, China, Nepal, Bangladesh, and Myanmar. Its population of 650,000 people consists of a few different ethnic groups. The first are called Ngalongs and come from the western mountains. The second are the Sharchhops—the Easterners—and the last are the Lhotshampas—the Southerners or the Nepali speaking Bhutanese. Almost all the refugees currently living in Nepal come from the last group. Before the crisis, about one-third to one-half of the total population were Nepali-speaking Southerners.

In 1958, Bhutan passed the first citizenship act. This enabled the entire southern Bhutanese population that had migrated to Bhutan between 1890 and 1920 to become citizens. Southerners could have jobs and grow food; however, they were not allowed to own land and there was very little interaction between the Southerners and the Northerners.

By the early 1980s, the government started to see the southern Bhutanese as a threat to the peaceful nation. In 1985, the second citizenship act was passed, and all the Southerners had to prove through documentation that they were legal residents. If not, they would be called non-national. This created civil unrest and protests by 1990. All those who participated in protests were arrested. During that time, thousands of southern Bhutanese were kept in detention centers in bad condition, and many of them were tortured during their incarceration. When some of them came out of the prison, they realized their houses had been destroyed, and their families were tortured and forced to leave Bhutan.

The refugees first fled to India but were not allowed to stay for a long time, and from there, they moved to East Nepal. In 1991, about six hundred refugees entered Nepal daily. By the end of 1992, around 80,000 refugees were living in camps set up by UNHCR. It is estimated that over 100,000 southern Bhutanese lost everything between 1990 and 1993, and Bhutan has not taken a single refugee back.

Next, I wanted to explore more about the Bhutanese refugees that were living in Nepal. So, I talked to a Nepali journalist who worked very closely with Bhutanese refugees. He was a sweet man with a great deal of knowledge about the refugee crisis in Nepal. He was a true journalist; a few times while talking to him, he would whisper and say, "Please shut the recorder for this part."

Here is my conversation with him:

Tell me about yourself?

I have been a journalist for many years covering mostly the refugees.

When did refugees start coming to Nepal?

The first batch of refugees came from Tibet in the early 1960s. According to the UNHCR, there are currently 24,000 Tibetan refugees living here. Most of the refugees that came from Tibet either live in Kathmandu or Pokhara. Another batch of refugees came from Bhutan in the early 1990s.

Why did the Bhutanese people leave their country?

Bhutanese people of Nepali descent were asked to leave. The government used civil unrest as a reason to expel people even though 99% of the people who fled had legal documents to stay in Bhutan. I know one man who was a member of parliament, and he was also forced to leave the country. Another man who was the physician for the Royal Family was also expelled.

Why do you think these people were expelled?

These people lived at the border of Nepal and Bhutan. They were getting an education and questioning human rights violations. These Southerners started demonstrating and protesting, so the government cracked down on them. Many of these people got murdered and raped. And because of that, many families were either expelled or fled to Nepal.

How did they get to Nepal?

In 1993, the UNHCR set up camps and tried to help people get settled who were coming through the borders. They were given shelter, food, and stipends. At that time, about 85,000 Bhutanese came to Nepal.

How did Nepal deal with so many refugees?

Nepal tried very hard to have talks with Bhutan from 1993 to 2001. They tried for the resettlement of these refugees, but the Bhutanese government was not willing to take them back.

Who were these 85,000 people?

These people can be divided into four categories. The first kind were the people who were forcefully expelled. The second group left on their own because they felt they were in danger. The third group of people was criminals, and the fourth was the undocumented people that were living in Bhutan.

How did you get involved with writing about refugees?

One of the camps was right next to my house. I remember riding my bike there. I always stopped and talked to the people living in the camps, and we created some great friendships.

What happened to all those refugees?

In 2006, after Nepal realized that Bhutan was not going to take any of the refugees back, it got help from the international community. Eight different countries including America, Australia, the UK, and Denmark, gave visas for the resettlement of these refugees. America took 86.6% of these refugees.

Has there been any recent efforts to send some of these refugees back?

About three to four months ago, the ministers from Bhutan and Nepal met to discuss this issue, and it seems like something might've been agreed upon. The UNHCR came up with the form last week for people who would like to go back to Bhutan.

***

My journalist friend had organized a meeting for me in which I got to speak with a refugee who left Bhutan and living in Nepal at the time.

I was a little nervous about this meeting, as everything seemed so mysterious as I had little to no information regarding the person. Our car followed my friend who rode his motorbike in front of us. He masterfully zigzagged through the narrow streets and my driver seemed to know exactly how to handle the traffic we were faced with.

We finally arrived at the refugee's house and reached the front of a small gate in a busy neighborhood. It was a tiny, compact two-story house, and Mr. Giri lived on the top floor. We climbed up the narrow stairs and were met with a curtain hanging in front of the door. My friend walked right in and called out Mr.

Giri's name. A tall man emerged from inside of the house. He was wearing a black leather jacket with a sweater underneath, making his hunchback even more prominent. My first impression of him was that he looked dejected and sad.

Still, he greeted us warmly, and we sat down. I took a moment to look around the room and noticed a variety of pictures covering the walls. Some were black and white, while others were of Mr. Giri as a young man in the army. There were a few that appeared recently. The walls of his living room told a story of their own; the pictures presented a life well lived and memories that haunted him.

As we began our conversation, he seemed excited to tell me his story. Giri talked more about how he became an outsider in his own country. The past haunted him and was more real compared to the present life that he was living. He urged me to share his story with the world.

Tell me about yourself?

My name is Giri from Bhutan. I went to primary school in Bhutan, and after that, I went to India to study. I came back to Bhutan after I graduated high school. I continued my higher education and got a degree in engineering from London.

What did you do after you got your degree?

I came back home and joined the army. I was an army officer for about ten years, and after that, the king personally assigned me to work on a project with UNICEF in central Bhutan. I moved there with my wife and two children in 1988. My life was perfect. I was truly blessed.

Then, suddenly, we felt like the environment started to change. People were talking about things, and because I was in the army, I could not get involved in any kind of conversations, nor could I even talk about these activities.

What was going on?

In 1990, everything changed for me. Things weren't good.

You keep on saying that things were happening, and people were having conversations. What are you referring to? Are you referring to the civil unrest or the citizenship act?

It was just stuff to create problems in Bhutan. One of our colleagues who later went on to become a very important person started to tell us what was going on in villages. He tried to get a reaction from us and find out our opinions about the civil unrest that was starting. He even asked me why I wasn't a part of Bhutan's People Party, which was the party creating the unrest and going against the king. He asked me if I would participate in demonstrations. I got very upset and told him my loyalties are with my country. The king had been very good to me, and I was not going to betray him.

So, who were these people at the Bhutan People's party?

I don't agree with anyone's opinion or what they wanted to do, but basically, they wanted everyone to live together in peace and harmony. They also didn't want the Southerners to be considered foreigners.

Then what happened?

The Bhutanese People's Party organized a huge demonstration; there were many people, and we had to shut down our office. It was September 1990. I was in charge of the security to make sure that everyone was safe. I was driving around in my car making sure no one was getting hurt. The demonstrations continued for a few days, and the police started to hurt people and raid their houses. They then converted an old hospital into a detention center. The police started to throw people in there.

How did you feel about that?

I started to get very upset because they were throwing eighty-year-old people or people who had nothing to do with the demonstrations into these detention centers. When I questioned them, they said that these people have been training militants. I didn't believe them because the kind of people they were arresting and torturing was harmless. I started to get upset at the police, and one of my friends told me, "Giri, stay out of it. Don't get involved. Don't say anything against it. Stay quiet."

At that time, my daughter was born, and I had to take my wife to a different city for delivery and recovery. After a few months, I came back, and things were pretty much the same. We were told to shut down our office and report back to the king. Everyone left, and I was in charge of closing the office and making sure everything was shut down.

Where did you go then?

We moved to another city and were settling in there. One evening, we had guests over for dinner. It was December 1990. There was a loud knock at the door. The army people forced themselves into my house, arrested me, and took me to the same detention center.

I kept asking them why they were taking me. They said it was because I was a traitor and the colonel said so. I told them I wasn't, but they put me in their car and took me to the detention center.

Did they ever tell you why they arrested you?

There were no charges; no one told me anything. I constantly shouted from my cell at the guards, asking them what I did.

At that moment, Mr. Giri's voice started to get shaky, and he had tears rolling down his face. I asked him if he wanted to stop for a bit, but he said no and wanted to continue.

How many people were in the detention centers?

About three hundred to four hundred people were in there. There were old people and children.

What was the worst thing about it?

That while I was in there, they harassed and tortured my wife and children. They took all the money from the bank and broke *everything in the house. My family was penniless; I don't know how they survived for over a year. Eventually, they were forced to leave the country. During the fourteen months that I was at the detention center, I had no idea where my family was, and they didn't know anything about me.*

What happened once you finally left the detention center?

I got out and went straight to my home; it was in awful shape. I went to see my elderly parents who hadn't left the country yet because they were waiting for me. My brother was also detained. He was a teacher. I was released on February 4th, 1992, and I left Bhutan on February 10th, 1992.

Where did you go?

I came to Nepal as a refugee. My family was in India, so I brought them here as well. My father passed away from the trauma; it was too much.

After my wife was tortured, she wasn't doing well. I tried my best to get her the best medical attention and take care of her. But she eventually died, and we are here now.

How many children do you have?

I have three children, and they are all doing well.

Do you ever wish to go back to Bhutan?

Of course, I want to go. I miss home, and I want to understand why things happened the way they did. The king should come forward and accept responsibility for what has happened to so many Bhutanese.

Do you feel as if this is your home, or Bhutan is your home?

I had never planned on coming to Nepal even though it is so close to Bhutan. I had been to India. But now it has been twenty-six years here. Bhutan will always be home. But I have remarried; my wife is Nepali, and she helps me financially, otherwise, I don't know how I would be able to survive.

***

Part Five

Southern California

I arrived back home on January 21ˢᵗ, 2019. I felt overloaded with information, and I had to write it all down; there was so much I wanted to say and explore but I felt tongue tied as I desperately tried to express my thoughts. So, I decided to talk to people who inspired me to take on this project because talking to them would help me clear my head. Maybe it was a selfish move, but I needed to understand my emotions better through these heroes.

The first person that came to my mind was my friend, Jackie Menter. She is the person that connected me with CESRT, Chios Eastern Shore Rescue Team. Below is my conversation with this inspirational woman:

Tell me a little about yourself.

I've worked in the non-profit sector for twenty years, spending most of those years at a human-relations and social services organization. The organization used a portion of funds toward humanitarian relief. Doing humanitarian aid work was always one of my life goals.

If you can use one word to describe yourself, what would it be? Why?

I would say "unstoppable." When I set a goal, I will do all it takes to attain it. The hardest part is overcoming my own fears and insecurities.

Why did you decide to do this work with refugees?

Humanitarian relief was a life goal I had not yet achieved. There was an opportunity in my life where I was no longer working full time; my children had completed high school, gotten driver's licenses, and were independent. During that time, my husband was also working full time and was in good health. So, I decided to pursue my goal of volunteering overseas to do aid work. This was just after the refugee crisis was receiving a lot of media attention and coverage after the death of Aylan Kurdi.

When did your work start?

I first went to Chios in June of 2016.

What have you learned about the refugee situation that you didn't know before working with them?

I really didn't know anything at all about the global refugee crisis before embarking on this journey. I have learned so much and have become a public speaker on the topic and a committed volunteer, both locally and abroad. My learning began with the Syrian refugee crisis, and I met many refugees while I was in Chios, Greece.

What did you learn from them?

I learned in the beginning not to ask why they left home and let them open that conversation when and if they chose to. I learned about their situations and their home lives before the war began in 2011. I've learned about the geography of Syria, as well.

Most importantly, I have learned about the tremendous resilience of refugees and what they had to give up and go through to get here. Every day, they are living in limbo in refugee camps or in a country not their own in search of a new homeland and to become integrated into a new society.

I have learned so much about the Syrian people and culture. I am amazed at their warmth and sincerity. I had never experienced such a degree of warmth and love from strangers. Their hospitality is incredible. Even if they don't know your name or speak your language, *they somehow find a way to make you feel at home. Even if home is a cold, damp tent with no heat, and even if they have nothing more to offer than the meager handouts from the camp, they still find a way to make you comfortable and welcome.*

I've also learned so much about migration and international asylum law, particularly how to attain asylum and benefits in Greece, Canada, and the US.

As a result, I have begun the process to become a DOJ accredited representative. When I finish the training, I will be recognized/ accredited to practice immigration law and represent asylum seekers in immigration court.

What is your best memory of working with refugee families?

I have so many good memories I don't know where to begin. One particularly striking facet of refugee life is that people have to leave members of their families behind or are left behind for a variety of reasons. Every refugee I have met has suffered tremendous loss, yet they continue.

The family bonds are stronger than I've seen before. People will do anything to protect and help their families, even if it means risking their own lives. And the family members back home will not share how devastating the situation is. They don't want the family member who has left to worry. And the refugee will not share how difficult and dangerous the journey was or how horrid the conditions are in which they now live. Each one protects the other.

How do you plan on raising awareness in your community about the refugee crisis?

I engage in public speaking and have organized multiple fundraisers and donation drives. A year ago, I co-founded the Orange County Jewish Coalition for refugees—a grassroots volunteer group that engages in advocacy, philanthropy, and raises awareness for refugees and asylum seekers.

What is the one thing people don't understand about refugee

families?

Refugees are people just like us. Many have a high degree of education (doctors, teachers, engineers, etc.) and have left good-paying jobs at home. Refugees are hardworking, resilient, brave, entrepreneurial people and will make great contributions to their new country. They are not religious radicals or terrorists. They are running from both those elements, have nearly all been personally persecuted, or have family members who have been killed, tortured, or disappeared (Syrians in particular).

If there was one thing you could change about the world today, what would it be?

Humanity and humility. People don't treat people well at all. We are cruel to each other.

Is there a solution to this crisis? Do you feel as though we are doing enough for people that have been displaced?

There are only political solutions. Governments do not want to solve this crisis. If they wanted to, it could be easily solved. We are definitely not doing enough, and most policies for migration and refugees are harmful to refugees and mainly set as deterrents. These policies don't work.

***

In 1951, the Refugee Convention declared, "Refugees are migrants who are able to demonstrate that they have been persecuted, or have reason to fear persecution, on the basis of one of five 'protected grounds': race, religion, nationality, political opinion, or membership in a particular social group."

America has a long history of providing security and help to people fleeing war and persecution. Nevertheless, in 1939, Congress stopped the bill that would let 20,000 German Jewish children into the US. Some people that were denied ended up in Nazi concentration camps in Europe and were tortured and killed. The US eventually changed its refugee policy, but not because of guilt over the Holocaust, rather it stemmed from concerns regarding the uncertainty of how Europe would look like post-World War II, as 20 to 30 million people had been displaced. Finally, in 1948, Congress passed the "Displaced Persons Act," which provided funding for the resettlement of refugees. However, the "country of origin quota" still existed, and Congress did not want to admit Jews and Eastern Europeans until the McCarran-Walter Act ended national origin quotas in 1952.

In 1953, Congress passed the refugee relief act, allowing over 200,000 immigrant visas to be provided to Europeans. In 1956, the US realized that people fleeing from communism would also be labeled as refugees. And so, in 1968, the US accepted the United Nations' definition of the term "refugee."

In 1970, 130,000 Vietnamese refugees resettled in the US. Between 1975 and 1978, the number of refugees entering the US drastically decreased. In 1970, 910,000 refugees from Vietnam came to the US. In 1980, Congress realized that there had to be a better way and procedure to allow refugees entrance and resettlement in the US. The Refugee Act of 1980 raised the annual ceiling for refugees from 17,400 to 50,000, created a process for reviewing and adjusting the refugee ceiling to meet emergencies, and required annual consultation between Congress and the president.

In 1980, there were over 200,000 arrivals—the highest number of refugee admissions in history. Eventually, the number decreased. There was a significant drop in refugee admissions because, after 9/11, the Bush administration stopped the refugee program for nearly two months because many refugees were coming from Somalia, Afghanistan, and Iraq—countries that had been infiltrated by Al Qaeda. Even though none of the 9/11 terrorists had come in on refugee visas, most of them were on tourist visas; four had a business visa and one had a student visa.

When President Obama was elected to office, he raised the cap to 85,000, and by the time he left, he had set it for 110,000 refugee admissions per year. Trump reduced the cap to 50,000, however the Biden administration increased that to 125,000 for the 2022 fiscal year.

Many of the families that come to the US seeking asylum or refugee status are detained. Currently, there are about 200 detention centers in the US. According to federal government data, Texas, California, Arizona, Georgia, and Louisiana have the largest number of detainees per day. The age range for the detainees varies. According to US government data, the median age of a person deported by ICE is thirty years old. According to the data collected by Freedom for Immigrants, most people in immigrant detention centers are between the ages of twenty-six to thirty-five.

The largest number of detainees come from Mexico, followed by El Salvador, Honduras, Guatemala, Haiti, and Ghana.

I talked to Jan Meslin, one of the founders of the organization called Friends of the Orange County Detainees. I have known Jan for years; she is a wonderful woman with short hair and a twinkle in her eye. I met her when I wanted to start visiting Muslim detainees about five years ago. It was difficult for me to see young men who were the same age as my son in the prisons; their families had no clue whether they were dead or alive. While completing this project, I thought of Jan numerous times. How did she stay strong and positive after hearing all those horrific stories? So, I decided to sit down and have a chat with her.

Tell me a little bit about yourself.

My name is Jan Maslin. I have always been an activist for women's rights, antiwar, single-payer healthcare, immigrant rights, and so much more.

Did you learn activism from your parents or was it something that just came as you grew older?

Both my parents were teachers, but I think I learned a little bit from my mother. I always had a sensitivity toward marginalized people.

How did you get involved in immigration-related activism?

I first got involved with an organization called CREER when I started to meet and befriend undocumented folks. The reason I became passionate about helping my friends in CREER is that lots of hate was being spewed against them by the Minutemen.

I also got involved with OCCCO, which is an interfaith organizing group that empowers community members and I started to attend City Council meetings to speak up for them.

What made you do that?

I saw how good these people were and how all they wanted was to protect their families. Eventually, some of the fathers were put in detention centers and deported.

That must've been very difficult.

We started to talk about it at my church. They came out with "Immigration as a Moral Issue," which is the Unitarian Universalist Association's Congregational Study/Action Issue (CSAI) 2010-2014. This study guide was created to help Unitarian Universalist congregations and individuals engage in the issue of immigration.

It was such a wonderful curriculum and the six-week program included:

1.   *Week One: Understanding the Causes of Migration*

2.   *Week Two: History of Immigration in the US*

3.   *Week Three: Economics of (Im)migration*

4.   *Week Four: Security, Enforcement, and Human Rights*

5.   *Week Five: Who Benefits from a Broken System?*

6.   *Week Six: Seeking Solutions*

The more I learned, the more I understood, and the more I felt a kinship to these people who left their homes behind in search of a better life.

So, were these asylum-seekers, or were they refugees?

There's not a lot of difference between asylees and refugees. It's just a procedural thing. They both leave their country for the same reason—in search of a place where their families will be safe. Asylees usually go straight into detention centers whereas refugees are supposed to be protected because of their status.

What did you do when you saw your friends being detained?

We created a group called the Friends of the Orange County Detainees. We went to these detention centers and talked to them. Some of them are locked up for years, and they have no one to talk to. The program is still going strong, and they have one hundred volunteers doing several thousand visits a year.

Are you still a part of it?

I stepped away from it because I wanted to get involved in changing the system. Now I work with Freedom for Immigrants; they have done a tremendous amount of work for the betterment of all kinds of immigrants. We are working on policies to abolish immigration detention, for better conditions for the detainees, a hotline, and a penal program.

Were you ever arrested?

I was arrested in 2010, along with about one hundred other people. About twenty-five were clergy.

What strikes you the most about these people?

It upsets me that they are such wonderful, talented people that could be valuable members of society, and they are locked up in jails. They are artists, musicians, engineers, teachers, and more. Some of them are locked up for an unknown amount of time. It's so unfair;

their families are hurting. Once, I remember a detainee told me that his kids wouldn't come to see him because it was so difficult for them to see their father behind a glass wall. He couldn't hug them, and it broke his heart.

Many people say that it's the fault of the people who come here and put their children through this. What do you say to them?

I can't imagine leaving my country or sending my kids away, but people are helpless. In Guatemala, young girls are forced into prostitution, young boys into gangs, and fathers are shot right there in front of their families. I feel like the US involvement in so many countries are also a cause of this. We have overthrown so many sitting presidents and installed military dictatorship for our own benefit. That is what we did in Honduras, and now it's the most dangerous country in the world. Everything changed for me when I got close to suffering. That's when I became more understanding of other people's problems.

Let me ask you this: You are a white woman—the privileged race. Why fight for others?

Because coming from my position of privilege, I can do it. Someone who is currently struggling with an issue can't do much because they are just trying to survive. From doing this work, I also realized that my country is based on racism. There was a time in history where the Pope made a decree that Native Americans could be killed because they weren't humans but savages, and to take over land as their discovery, and do with Natives as they pleased because they were heathens. Then, there was slavery. My race benefits from all this history of oppression and racism.

For example, my father was in the army, and when he came back, he was able to benefit from the GI bill and go back to school because he was a white man. If he were black, he wouldn't be able to. He was a teacher, and so was my mom. I benefitted from this.

I truly believe that when anybody is suffering, we are all suffering. Just like Martin Luther King said, "It's not over until everybody gets justice. Our lives are connected with each other."

How can we bring change?

I believe our whole system needs to be changed.

***

According to the California Department of Social Services, between 2013 and 2017, refugees came from the following countries:

Afghanistan: 1,111

Middle East/Iraq[1]: 13,269

Iran: 8,510

Former USSR[2]: 2,936

Southeast Asia[3]: 1,323

Africa[4]: 3,250

Other[5]: 883

Total: 31,282

***

Through my friend, Jackie Menter, I met a refugee from Cameroon who came to the US in 2017. Below is my conversation with him:

Tell me about yourself.

I am from Cameroon, and I arrived at the US border on February 23rd, 2017. I belong to the Banso tribe in the Anglophone region of Cameroon.

Why did you have to leave Cameroon?

I had to leave Cameroon because of political reasons.

Why did you have to leave? Specifically, how was it a threat to you?

Cameroon is composed of two different regions; the bigger region was colonized by the French and the smaller by the British. When they came together as one country, the president divided the country into ten regions. Out of those, eight regions were French-speaking and two were English-speaking. Priority was always given to the Francophone communities. In October of 2016, the lawyers in the Anglophone regions protested against the government to stop appointing French-speaking magistrates who did not know any English. None of the laws were translated into English, and teachers coming to the Anglophone regions were also French speakers who spoke little or no English, sidelining the importance of the Anglophone people. After the lawyers, the teachers came out to strike for the same reason. They were brutally beaten and hurt.

Are you a teacher or a lawyer?

No, I was a business owner, and we decided to support the lawyers and teachers. On October 1st, we decided to shut down the whole market and protest peacefully on the streets. The military forces were sent out, and they fired shots at us. Many people were hurt or killed. I was very lucky that I got out safe and sound.

At that moment, I realized that I could never be safe in my own country. The military started arresting young people and throwing them in jails for no reason at all. They were targeting the youth because they realized that is what would make us weaker and would destabilize our region.

What did you decide to do?

The next morning, there was chaos in my city. The military forces were breaking into people's houses, beating them up, and taking their young people to jail. I knew I had to leave the city. As I was trying to run away at 4:00 a.m., I got caught by one of the military guys, and he told me to lie down on the mud. I asked him why and told him that I *had done nothing. I was trying to communicate with him, and at that moment, he hit me really hard on my mouth. I fell down and started to bleed all over. I started to shiver because it was very cold and there was blood everywhere. The military guys thought that I was dying, and they picked me up and took me to the hospital.*

The hospital was also chaotic. People were running, crying, and the military was everywhere. The military was trying to tell people to calm down, and they would constantly shoot bullets in the air so that people would do as they said. The doctor tried to sew my lip. The doctor left the room because he heard something and at that moment, I realized that this was my chance to run away. I knew that was the only moment I could escape, or they would eventually throw me in prison and build a huge case against me that would not even be true. I got up, jumped off the bed, went to the corridor, and ran outside to the street. Once I was away from the hospital, I stopped a car.

The man in the car was very helpful. He told me to be careful because now that I had escaped the hospital, they would be looking for me everywhere. He said that I should go to Nigeria and then figure out where to go from there. I asked if he could help me get transportation to take me to Nigeria. He was very helpful and arranged everything for me.

He was like an angel!

Yes, he was like an angel; he was extremely helpful. They put me in the luggage section on public transportation. They would bribe the people at the checkpoints so they would not check the luggage compartment and I would have to pay that bribe.

What happened when you finally got to the border?

When I got to the border, I stayed with the family for a little while. But then I needed my papers because if I entered Nigeria illegally, then I would never be able to get asylum anywhere.

A section of the border is an extremely dangerous jungle, and there was a lot of checking going on at the border. During the time that I waited to get all my paperwork together, I hid in the jungle and came out to get my papers that my mom had been sending through the driver.

How long did it take you to get your papers?

It took me about two months to get everything, and I was able to enter Nigeria legally. From Nigeria, I could go to Ecuador because there is no visa required there. But there was no direct flight from Nigeria to Ecuador, so I had to take a ferry to Senegal. The journey from Nigeria to Senegal took three days, and from Senegal, I got to Ecuador. From Ecuador, I went to Columbia, and then I ended up in a refugee camp in Panama. From there, I went to Costa Rica and was in another refugee camp.

What difference do you see between the different refugee camps?

In the refugee camps, they don't want people to stay, so they intentionally treat them like they are nothing. Every camp is horrible. At the camp, there were no bathrooms. We had to shower in the river; we were sleeping in tents that were full of mosquitoes and bugs.

From Costa Rica, we got to the US border and we were arrested. I was sent to a detention center for nine months.

How do you stay so strong?

What can I do? My biggest goal was to survive each day. When I was in the worst of situations, the only thing I could think of was how I would stay alive for that day. I didn't know what would happen at any given moment, and so I just learned to survive and move forward.

What happened at the detention center?

When I had my first hearing, the judge asked me if I had anyone to represent me. I told him I had no family, no friends, and didn't know anyone. He gave me a list of pro bono attorneys, and once I got back to my cell, I wrote to each one of them. Finally, one of them agreed to take my case, and he worked hard for me. I was granted asylum on

November 9th, 2018.

Once I got out, I had nowhere to go, so my lawyer connected me with an organization that helped me find a place to live.

So, in your journey from the time of the protests in Cameroon until the time you left the detention center, what was the scariest moment?

I think the scariest time for me was my journey from Ecuador to the US border.

Now that you are here, and you have your whole future ahead of you, what would your dream life be like ten years from now?

I would want to be in a place where I can help people be happier and more fulfilled. If there's one thing I've learned, it's that life can end in a split second, and it's so important to be happy, be at peace, and follow your dream.

What is the worst thing that you saw at the refugee camps?

I saw that they intentionally demolish your existence and diminish you to nothingness. You feel like you mean nothing, but what they need to understand is that people like me would never leave a country if things were better there. We are running from something scarier and bigger than all of us.

***

Since 2007, San Diego County has taken in the most refugees in California. In 2016, about 3,100 refugees were resettled in San Diego County, and the number sharply dropped by a little over 50% in 2017, which saw the resettlement of 1,500 refugees. As mentioned earlier, President Trump decreased the cap for the number of refugees entering the country from 110,000 to 50,000. This caused court cases, implementation of travel bans, and stopped people who had the necessary paperwork from entering the country, despite the fact that they have been waiting for years. This caused resettlement agencies, community organizations, and other non-profit organizations to scramble to help these refugees.

One such organization in San Diego is The Episcopal Refugee Network—a non-profit organization that has been helping the refugee community for over twenty years. They assist refugees in the resettlement process, which includes learning a new language, adapting to a new culture, and finding a way to support themselves. They provide tutoring for about one hundred young refugees three days a week. Students are placed in sections based on age rather than knowledge. They are taught and get to practice reading skills, math skills, and receive help with homework.

Tell me a little about yourself.

I'm a father, an educator, an immigrant, a Christian, a music-lover, a world traveler, a skeptic, a procrastinator, and a seeker.

If you could use one word to describe yourself, what would it be? Why?

Curious. Because I use Wikipedia about fifty times a day as I always want to know more about things that I hear about, anything that sparks my interest and passion.

Why did you decide to do this work with refugees?

I had an acquaintance, Marilyn Nahas, who was an Episcopalian like me, and she ran a tutoring program for refugees. She was the person who encouraged me to attend and volunteer. We became great friends—an Englishman in his forties and a former Texas beauty pageant winner in her late seventies. She inspired me. And I fell in love with the children from Myanmar, and the South Sudanese children, and the boys and girls from the Congo—the newest Americans among us.

When did you start working with refugees?

About seven or eight years ago.

What have you learned about the refugee situation that you didn't know before working with them?

The lack of empathy that so many people show—their ancestors were immigrants and refugees, and America welcomed them and gave them a new life and opportunities—and yet they selfishly seek to deny that to others.

Your best memory of working with refugee children?

The Holiday Gift Drives we organize, and the Cultural Exchange one of my students arranged last year when refugee children visited our school, played sports, and did crafts with our students, shared pizza and cookies, made kites, then went down to the beach next to school (many of them had never been to the ocean) and flew their kites, which was like a metaphor for their little souls, taking flight, catching the wind, soaring into the heavens.

How do you plan to raise awareness in your community about the refugee crisis?

I do all that I can to encourage students at my school to volunteer in our program and raise awareness and support among their parents. My church is also made up of greater than fifty percent refugees and does a lot of advocacy and community service work among that population. Jesus was a refugee in Egypt. The Jews were often persecuted refugees in foreign lands. Prophet Muhammed was a refugee in Yathrib / Medina. Lord Ram was exiled to the forest in the Ramayana. Siddhartha Gautama Buddha was a refugee in India when his home kingdom in Nepal was suffocating and unwelcoming.

What is the one thing people don't understand about refugee families?

How hard they work, how much they have endured, what they have escaped from, and the effort and energy it takes to get here, to fight the system to be recognized and accepted.

If there was one thing you could change about the world today,

what would it be?

Introduce a policy of conscripted community service for everyone—two years of serving your community, at home or abroad, in exchange for free college tuition.

Is there a solution to this crisis? Do you feel as though we are doing enough for people that have been displaced?

No and No. Not until human nature evolves beyond the desire for power, domination, and selfish aggrandizement; not until we learn to steward the fragile resources of the earth, not until we learn to treat others as we would want to be treated.

***

Reaching the US on asylum is one thing, but resettlement is another. Adjustment is difficult for refugees who arrived in a new country where they are perceived to be the *other*, where language competency is low, socio-economic conditions are bad, and the trauma of war still resides in them. It is hard for families to navigate everything that they would need, including a home, jobs, getting kids in school, obtaining a driver's license, and more.

I spoke to my friend, Ana, who has helped many people in the resettlement phase. She has done this work for years, and being an immigrant herself, she understands how these people feel. I was lucky enough to work firsthand with Anna in Chios, Greece, and her dedication is remarkable.

Tell me about yourself.

I was born in Argentina and moved to Brazil when I was seven years old. Then, I eventually moved back to Argentina. I finally came to the US about thirty-two years ago. All the moving around helped me develop compassion for people from every walk of life, ethnicity, and race.

If you could use one word to describe yourself, what would it be? Why?

It's hard to say one, so I will use three: connection seeker, helper, and cheerleader.

Why did you decide to do this work with refugees?

I have always liked to help people and volunteer with different organizations. Last year, I got the opportunity to work in Chios, Greece. While I was there, I learned firsthand the difference one person can make—how we all have the power in ourselves to organize a movement and help others. I also realized that I have to do my part in helping others in need. I think it is very easy to sit back and judge others, but it is so important to jump in and help people in need.

What have you learned about the refugee situation that you didn't know before working with them?

I realized that all this is about money and politics.

What is the one thing people don't understand about refugee families?

That we perceive them as the others at any given time.

Tell me a story about a family you helped.

The family I helped was from Central America. There were two parents and three children. The mother spoke a little bit of Spanish, but the father didn't as they lived in the outskirts of a small town and spoke a different dialect. The oldest son, who was fifteen, had been kidnapped and trafficked but was able to escape while living in Central America. The family decided to leave because they feared for their child's safety. Once they arrived at the border, they were put in a detention center. Eventually, they got their asylum approved and have been working with an organization for resettlement.

I was able to help the family find an apartment and a full-time job with benefits for the father. The father didn't like his first job as the language was a barrier, so I helped him find another job. I also helped him find an apartment and got the kids enrolled in school.

The struggles that the family faced were that they didn't speak the language, they felt isolated from the community, and the oldest child had no access to mental health help. The younger two were dealing with the trauma of leaving their home and being at the detention centers. I saw this trauma very clearly in the whole family, and I understood that the road to recovery was very long. The parents did not understand the life here; they didn't know what to expect when their children went out of the house. What do they choose, feeling displaced or the safety of their child?

***

When thinking of a massive human tragedy as significant as the refugee crisis, there is another aspect to it. Many businesses and individuals are taking advantage of people in despair. They are monetizing the crisis and making a huge profit. War isn't just a political step; it is also a business, which in turn creates displaced people who need to flee. Many governments and private corporations benefit from this through reconstruction businesses, housing, medical treatment, and more. On a smaller level, store owners charge extra for cell phones, food, water, and necessities. As previously mentioned, before the journey begins, the refugees are sold life vests that are made of plastic and are fake.

The journey that refugees embark on is not only deadly but also poses a risk for them to become entangled in sex trafficking rings. Sometimes, they willingly accept to take on sex work, as it doesn't require any paperwork or knowledge of the language. They see it as a means of financial stability, and smugglers promise that the sex work would be profitable. Many refugees have no other options of making money. However, once they are lured in, they are treated as sex slaves and are abused.

Children currently make up more than half the refugee population. Often, parents send their children alone, or they get separated during the journey. According to the European Union's criminal intelligence agency, Europol, in 2016, at least tens of thousands of unaccompanied refugee children went missing. Around 5,000 were missing in Italy and around 1,000 in Sweden. The Europol has seen a direct connection between traffickers that smuggle refugees and those that are profiteering from selling them into sex and slavery.

Migration is a lucrative business for prisons, immigration detention centers, and housing for these refugees. Immigration detention centers need staff, guards, personnel, buildings, guns, and so much money is made by either public or private prisons. Prisons have become a huge money-making business.

Many people hear these stories and believe that people should live in their own countries and wonder why they come here in the first place. Some of them sit in detention centers for years before a judge will hear their case. There are so many atrocities that happen in these detention centers—there is a serious abuse of power and no respect for the inmates.

I interviewed Gretta, a transgender woman who came here looking for asylum. Gretta's story is horrific and heartbreaking and is the story of thousands of others. When I called Gretta, she was positive and cheerful; truly inspirational.

So wonderful to connect with you, tell me about yourself.

My name is Gretta, and I'm a forty-five-year-old transgender woman. I came to the US about fourteen years ago from Mexico seeking asylum. I came here alone in 2003, but I have found a new family here.

How was your journey coming to the US?

It was a very difficult journey. It took about fifteen days to get to the Arizona state border. Every time we heard the border patrol, we hid and sat still for hours. This slowed our journey. While walking, many people bumped into cacti and got thorns all over their bodies. Others were stung by insects and got very sick. There were ants everywhere, and they would climb all over us, but we couldn't scream or shout from the pain because border patrol was everywhere.

When we got to the border and took off our shoes, our feet had been damaged; they were scratched and had blisters from walking so much in the heat.

How big was the group you came with?

It was a group of about fifty people. The man who was taking us told us that we had to continue to walk no matter what. If there was someone who was sick, old, or tired and couldn't walk anymore, he would leave them. They would be given a lighter or a matchbox, and we would collect some dry wood and leave the person there with a little fire pit. He did that so the border patrol could find them and take them instead of them dying in the desert. By the time we got to the border, we realized that more than half the group had been left behind. It was really difficult to leave people behind. When we saw smoke somewhere, we knew it was someone waiting to be picked up by border patrol.

So, do you think it was worth all the pain?

Wow, that's a really difficult question. As much as I feared my safety back home, that was home. I miss my friends; I miss the life I had. Even though back home I had to hide my identity as a transgender woman, here I feel like a slave. I have been trying to get my papers in order. I hardly have any rights. I can't take a vacation; whatever I earn, I pay toward bills. So, all I'm doing today is surviving.

I am also very lucky because I have some amazing women that are helping me, and I've also become an activist to help other transgender women. When I look at some trans women across the border, I see that in order to survive, they have to do whatever they can to pay their bills; some of them are forced to take up prostitution. And this issue puts trans women in a bad situation where they're constantly sexually harassed and raped, and no one is willing to stand up for them.

What are the hardships you think people coming to this

country face?

Firstly, people that come here have a language barrier. Secondly, it's very expensive to survive here, and it's hard to make a living if you can't speak the language properly. Education is also a factor. Sometimes people don't have enough education to move forward. That's why I am going back to school to better myself.

So, you're going to school. What are you studying?

I'm studying to get my GED, and I am currently on my third level of ESL and also studying math.

Have you had to deal with any kind of discrimination being a Mexican, asylum-seeking, transgender woman?

Generally, people have been okay, but sometimes it does happen. Like for example, about four days ago, I went to my doctor, and they constantly called me by my male name. I have requested them many times to call me Gretta, but they don't. It's embarrassing for me. I understand that my legal name still hasn't been changed, but if I have told them again and again, I feel like they should show some respect.

Do you think people do it intentionally or they just don't care?

I think they just don't care, and they don't realize that they are disrespecting others.

Were there other instances of people discriminating against you?

There are many instances that I can recall. I don't know if it's because I am considered an outsider, or because I'm a trans woman. But one thing I know for sure is that when people think you are an outsider, it's like fighting a monster—a monster that holds all the power like David and Goliath.

Epilogue

Coming back home to Orange County, California and reflecting on what I had witnessed was hard. But despite how I felt, it was time to put this all together. I went into this project thinking I would know more, but now I feel even more lost and less knowledgeable. I feel confused and insignificant compared to what's happening in the world. It is something that can't be described in words. Still, let me try.

Before my travels, I felt incredibly excited, but once I arrived for the interviews, my heart sank every time. Then, I saw and felt the warmth of those I was surrounded by, and my heart smiled. But as their stories were told, I felt pessimistic and angry about the injustice they had witnessed.

During my travels, I saw many things, some of which made sense, while others didn't. But there was one common thread: I saw joy and endurance reside within despair and agony. I felt optimism amid melancholia and happiness among people who had lost everything. It was a weird feeling that I couldn't quite put my finger on.

The pain of others affected me. After some interviews, I couldn't sleep, and insomnia became a part of my routine. I walked around feeling the trauma of others. I visualized their stories while writing about them. Maybe it was my writer's brain, or maybe their pain was so enormous that it engulfed me. I saw so many children that had been affected by displacement. Some of them were oblivious to the dire conditions their families were in. They played like other children while their mothers watched over them with joy. In some children, I saw the trauma in their eyes

—a mixture of sadness, fear, and hope. It was the same with the adults. Some had the spark for the future still in them as their eyes lit up when they spoke or they had a bounce of confidence in their step as they walked. Others trudged forward with hunched backs, hands tightly clasped, and a hollowness in their eyes that no living being should have. There were so many days when I felt their trauma and my own past aired its head like an ugly monster. But little did I realize the impact of working in the non-profit sector and taking in other people's pain for seven years would have on me, especially as I was already struggling with a form of PTSD. I was hearing horrific stories from my clients, and they lived on inside me.

As I finished my journey that started in October of 2017 and collected all my thoughts, the feeling was bittersweet. I started this journey because I wanted to know so many things. I didn't know how I would get the funding or how I would be able to travel and get in touch with people, but it happened. Things just fell in place. Before leaving, I even got to spend time with the amazing poet, Carolyn Forsche, who gave me guidance on how to talk to people who have been through the trauma of war. I was able to find teachers who encouraged and supported me and my family who, despite thinking I was crazy, cheered me on.

Traveling to four different countries and talking to so many people about the refugee situation has made me realize many things about myself. Someone once asked me why I sympathize so much with refugees, and whether it is worth spending so much of my time going to places and talking to them.

My answer is yes; it was worth it.

Is it worth spending all that money to go into unknown territories, just to learn more?

Yes.

Some of my friends even wanted me to share my location with them in case I got kidnapped. I just smiled and said, "I've lived in Orange County; I can handle anything."

Yes, I do feel a kinship with refugees. There have been many times in my life when I felt my home was taken away from me. Whether by choice or through circumstances beyond my control, I felt displaced in the sense that I felt vulnerable and naked. My home, my security—no matter what it was—disappeared, and I had to search for a new one.

The first moment I felt displaced was when my parents decided to move back to Pakistan when I was seven years old. Today, I believe it was one of the best decisions they made, but not so much at that time. I was born in Los Angeles County and grew up in Orange County until one day I found out that we were packing everything and moving. We were leaving for a country I had heard about, seen in pictures, and had seen my mother cry about many times, but I had no clue or concept of what it was.

I remember feeling absolutely uncanny when we landed at the airport in Pakistan. So many of our relatives had come to receive us. My mother hugged everyone and cried with joy, and my father smiled, laughed, and appeared happy. Everyone hugged me too, but I didn't know who they were. I smiled shyly the whole time and just stayed close to my sisters. At that moment, I felt lost and alone in such a large group of people who were excited to see my family and me.

For my parents, it was home.

But I was displaced and lost.

Pretty soon after arriving, we started school. I was in third grade. Living in the US, I never learned Urdu—Pakistan's national language—which made it even worse because I had no clue what people were saying. There was always kindness in their eyes and joy in their smiles, but their words were foreign to me. The first day of school, my mother gave us some new outfits to wear with green shorts and a white sleeveless top that had some flowers on it. It was an all-girl school, but because we were new, we were given a few days to get our uniforms.

I recall walking into school behind my older sister who was always motherly toward me. She accompanied me to my class and walked away. As I entered the class, a few girls looked at me and giggled. One girl approached me and said something, but I had no clue what it was. The teacher told me where to sit, and I obeyed. I remember that day very clearly. The other girls kept on calling me *angraiz*. I felt lost, alone, and sad. I believed the word was a bad one that meant dumb or stupid. Eventually, I realized that *angraiz* meant white person.

It took years to finally settle in and feel as though I belonged, but little did I know that displacement would follow me throughout my life.

My life became a series of events instead of a life lived to its fullest. I felt alone and vulnerable that day. There was a girl who was a bully. She would take my lunch every day. The day I found the courage to tell her to stop, the incident happened. I was walking from the playground to the class and felt a push. I fell to the floor, and she pulled off my glasses, threw them on the floor next to me, and stepped on them until they broke; she punched me and then casually grabbed my lunch and walked away. That was the day I knew school wasn't a safe place for me. And it was never a place where I felt at home.

The next time was when I was in 7th grade and had just changed schools. My mother decided that I should be in a better school and so I changed schools. Once again, I was displaced in the unknown.

At my old school, I didn't have friends, but at least I was familiar with the surroundings and could identify all the bullies. I knew exactly where I could hide and be safe. I knew that the bullies only bothered me when I was in front of them.

"Come here, Shaky (from Shaikh, my last name). Show me what you have for lunch."

"Can you still see?" one of them said as they pulled off my glasses and threw them far away.

"She is so stupid that even stupid people think she is more stupid." They burst into laughter.

But I was used to them and their ways; it had become part of my life.

However, in this new school, I was scared. I felt unsafe and out of place. This wasn't my home. Once again, I entered the unfamiliar territory and became an outsider, chained to a place that wasn't mine.

The school was huge. It looked something out of an old, British movie. We were told every day how the school was created in 1876, and how we should be grateful for being in such a prestigious institution. As we walked away from our morning assembly, the nuns checked our nails and shoes. I always got in trouble because I was a nail-biter. Every day, one of the nuns pulled me to the side, which was where they would send girls with nail polish, broken nails, or unladylike hands. The ones with unpolished shoes stood with us, too. After everyone left for class, we were lectured about how we were an embarrassment to the school and to our parents. Shame was supposedly a big motivator. When I finally got to my class after the lecture, my teacher rolled her eyes while the students giggled and whispered.

Every day as I walked through the school halls, I felt horrible. I wanted to be seen. Noticed. Both my sisters who were also in the same school already had friends and were happy, but I wasn't.

One day, as I was dropped off at school, I didn't wait outside with the rest of the girls for the morning assembly. Instead, I walked toward the back of the school into the bathroom. I stood in the doorway for a bit. I had come in to wash my face and just waste time before I had to face everyone out there. I sauntered across the stalls and entered the last one, slowly opening the door. I walked into the stall and looked around. At that moment, I thought to myself, "What would happen if I just stayed here? Maybe no one will find me."

I put my backpack beside the toilet and sat on the floor with my back toward the door. Then, it hit me that someone might see me if I sat like that, so I moved toward the side wall and put my legs on top of the toilet. I pulled out a book, *Oliver Twist,* and started to read. Life around me went on; the school bell continued to ring at regular intervals. A few girls came and used the other stalls. I heard water gushing out from the tap. After a couple of hours, I went out and walked around the bathroom a bit, then went back to my stall—my sanctuary. I stayed there until the end of the school day, then quietly picked up my bag and walked to the pickup area. My car came, and I went home.

I did this for a week, and no one noticed.

I walked into the school every day along with my sisters and other girls who were in my class. I even ran into some teachers and nuns as I walked in and out of the bathroom, but no one realized that I wasn't in class.

I was invisible, lost, and displaced.

***

Many people asked me if my connection with refugees is because my parents were immigrants, or because I have worked in the non-profit world and am sympathetic toward them. But I don't think that's the case. My parents came to the US in 1965, and my father wasn't forced to leave his home. He had worked as a professor at a prestigious university in Pakistan. He chose to migrate, and he had a country to go back to where his parents' home still stands. He traveled back and forth as he wanted and has now retired there. These are luxuries that refugees don't have, and I am grateful for the benefits I have every day because my parents were able to migrate legally.

I thought about ways to help refugees on a broader level; I wondered what I could do to raise awareness in my own area.

But then I felt so small. I still don't have an answer; I still feel lost, and the nightmares continue. I compared my displacement to that of people who lost everything. People who leave their homes, families, friends, and everything they know to go into unfamiliar territory. Some leave as families, while others come individually. Some send their children alone.

But displacement is an interesting word. It means something that is out of its "place," which in the case of the refugees, means they are physically away from their home. Most of them bring what they can and leave the majority of their belongings behind, things that we value and keep for years and years. So, can being physically away from everything that is familiar to you bring the feeling of emotional displacement? Does physical and emotional displacement go hand in hand?

Let's look at the word displacement again. It means being compelled to leave a place. Today, about 82.4 million people are displaced from their homes, out of which more than one-third are forced to leave because of war. To better understand the enormity of the situation, it's important to note that the population of the UK is 67.2 million and that the population of France is 67.3 million imagine half the population of Japan leaving—that is how many people have been forced to leave their home. We understand physical displacement as a crisis, but then what about its twin sister? What is the cost of emotional displacement? Many of us feel as if we don't or haven't belonged one or more times in our lives. This could be in school, among friends, in big gatherings, at university, at work, or in life in general. Some among us always feel out of place and lost, while others can feel at home anywhere. Being a part of a loving family doesn't necessarily mean that the feeling of belonging is there; people can still feel lost and displaced. It can take a lifetime to find a group or place to belong to.

So, is it the opposite of being displaced being at home? Home is supposed to be the place where we are most comfortable;

however, home is just defined as a place of residence. That's it. Nothing more.

But as humans, we associate home with peace and happiness. It is a place we come to at the end of the day where we can be ourselves and live our dream lives. Home is supposed to be a safe place. Many poets and writers have helped in romanticizing what home is. Poems like *Journey Home* by Rabindranath Tagore are examples of this:

The time that my journey takes is long and the way of it is long.

I came out on the chariot of the first gleam of light, and pursued my

voyage through the wildernesses of worlds leaving my track on many a star and planet.

It is the most distant course that comes nearest to thyself,

and that training is the most intricate which leads to the utter simplicity of a tune.

The traveler has to knock at every alien door to come to his own,

and one has to wander through all the outer worlds to reach the innermost shrine at the end.

My eyes strayed far and wide before I shut them and said, `Here art thou!'

The question and the cry, `Oh, where?' melt into tears of a thousand

streams and deluge the world with the flood of the assurance.

What is home?

If the opposite of being displaced is being at home, then what is home?

Is home just a place we live in?

Is it in the company of others that we feel at home?

Is it a period in our lives that we believed we were happy?

Is it a place we buy and pay for to live the rest of our lives?

Is it a piece of land that we farm and grow fruits and vegetables?

Is it any place we feel safe in?

Is it being around loved ones?

Growing up, every time my mom heard the song, "Country Roads" by John Denver, she cried. Even though her home was a small town in Pakistan and had nothing to do with West Virginia, it took her to a place where she remembered being happy and at peace—where she lived a life of innocence.

When we feel we are not at home because of loneliness, anxiety, and despair, can it be as harmful to our soul as it is for the refugees in war? I think the difference is that refugees struggle with physical displacement along with emotional trauma. They have lost their country and their sense of security.

For me home, has always been where I feel at peace and can be myself. I don't look at home in terms of time, but I know many people do. They try to recreate the magic they once felt at a certain time in their lives—a time when they belonged and were happy.

So, the question is, is displacement inevitable? We all move around in our lives to new houses, schools, countries, social circles, and more. We all grow as individuals where the old path becomes irrelevant, and we take on new journeys. Every new journey brings up a feeling of inadequacy and it takes time to accept the new road where life has taken us. We all have to leave the comfort of our homes and social circles to move ahead in life.

Refugees are people who are forced to leave for fear of being persecuted; however, others leave the past behind and move to greener pastures in search of more fulfillment, money, social status, or even to begin a family.

So, I still wonder, are we all refugees of some kind?

[1] Includes Iraq, Jordan, Lebanon, Syria, and Yemen.

[2] Includes Armenia, Azerbaijan, Belarus, Georgia, Kazakhstan, Kyrgyzstan, Latvia, Moldova, Russia, Tajikistan, Turkmenistan, Ukraine, and Uzbekistan.

[3] Includes Bhutan, Cambodia, India, Myanmar (Burma), Thailand, and Vietnam.

[4] Includes Burundi, Cameroon, Central African Republic, Congo (and Zaire), Cote D'Ivoire, Eritrea, Ethiopia, Gambia, Kenya, Liberia, Rwanda, Sierra Leone, Somalia, Sudan (and S. Sudan), and Uganda.

[5] Other includes Bangladesh, Brazil, Bulgaria, China, Columbia, Cuba, Egypt, El Salvador, Guatemala, Honduras, Indonesia, N. Korea, Kuwait, Nepal, Pakistan, Palestine, Senegal, S. Africa, Sri Lanka, Sweden, Tunisia, Unknown, and West Bank.

www.ingramcontent.com/pod-product-compliance
Lightning Source LLC
Chambersburg PA
CBHW051819250726

48659CB00005B/1573